Coping with the Psychologica

D0491191

Professor Robert Bor, DPhil, CPsychol, CSci, FBPsS, UKCP Reg, FRAeS, is a Chartered Clinical, Counselling and Health Psychologist registered with the Health Professions Council as well as a Family Therapist. He is the Consulting Psychologist at two of the UK's leading cancer treatment and research centres, the London Oncology Clinic and the London Clinic. In the NHS, he is the Lead Consultant Psychologist in Medical Specialties at the Royal Free Hospital in London. Rob has a very busy private therapy practice based in North and Central London, trading as Dynamic Change Consultants. He is a Fellow of the British Psychological Society, a member of the American Psychological Association, Institute of Family Therapy and the American Association for Marital and Family Therapy. Rob's expertise and experience is in helping children, young people and adults cope with cancer in the family. He works therapeutically with individuals, couples and families, drawing on modern, evidence-based psychological approaches. He is also the Consulting Psychologist to St Paul's School, JFS and the Royal Ballet School, all in London. He is an active member of the International Psycho-Oncology Society. Rob has published more than 170 articles and chapters in books as well as 25 books. He teaches communications skills to medical and nursing students. Rob is a Churchill Fellow.

Dr Carina Eriksen, MSc, DPsych, C.Psychol, BABCP acc, is an experienced Counselling Psychologist with a specific interest in helping individuals, couples and families deal with cancer-related concerns. Carina works in the NHS as well as in private practice. She provides therapy to adults, adolescents, children and families, drawing on her speciality within Cognitive Behavioural Therapy and Systemic Orientations. She is a Chartered Member of the British Psychological Society and an Accredited Member of the British Association for Behavioural and Cognitive Psychotherapies. She is a senior lecturer in Psychology at Roehampton University. Carina is an author and a co-author of several books and her work has been published in scientific journals.

Ceilidh Stapelkamp is a health research analyst with a special interest in public health. Ceilidh has an honours degree in Genetics and Microbiology and has completed a programme of post-graduate courses in Public Health, including Epidemiology, Statistics, Infectious Diseases and Evidence-based Medicine, at the London School of Hygiene and

Tropical Medicine. She was recently awarded a Master's in Public Health from King's College School of Medicine in London where she undertook research into the survival of women with breast cancer in the UK. Ceilidh has lectured with the Open University, has been involved in primary mental health research and was an NHS programme coordinator for a project to deliver child and adolescent community mental health services in Camden.

Overcoming Common Problems Series

Selected titles

A full list of titles is available from Sheldon Press,
36 Causton Street, London SW1P 4ST and on our website at
www.sheldonpress.co.uk

Overcoming Common Problems Series

Overcoming Common Problems Series

Overcoming Common Problems

Coping with the Psychological Effects of Cancer

PROFESSOR ROBERT BOR, DR CARINA ERIKSEN
& CEILIDH STAPELKAMP

RESS
ɔn

First published in Great Britain in 2010

Sheldon Press
36 Causton Street
London SW1P 4ST

British Library Cataloguing-in-Publication Data
A catalogue record for this book is available from the British Library

ISBN 978-1-84709-097-3

1 3 5 7 9 10 8 6 4 2

Typeset by Fakenham Photosetting Ltd, Fakenham, Norfolk
Printed in Great Britain by Ashford Colour Press

Produced on paper from sustainable forests

Contents

This book is dedicated to our patients and their families, and to all those professionals who care for people with cancer, as well as to our own families

1

Introduction and overview

Any illness can pose significant physical, emotional and practical challenges but, for some, cancer can be one of the hardest to bear. A diagnosis of cancer can wreak havoc in a person's life, affecting all aspects of functioning and daily living such as work, recreation, relationships, routines and habits, and of course how we feel in ourselves. Cancer can have a negative impact on self-confidence, mood, identity, capability, sleep and capacity for sexual intimacy. These are just a few of the possible psychological effects.

A diagnosis of cancer can be life-changing and in some cases can also prove life-threatening. We have seen through our professional experience that these are not overstatements. Of course, every person's situation is unique. Different health problems affect people in both obvious and unexpected ways. Exactly what effect they do have depends on your age and stage of life; your gender and role in a family; past and current patterns of relationship with your family; the nature of your medical problems and how they affect you; your relationship with professionals such as doctors, nurses and other caregivers; your ideas and experiences of coping with illness; as well as personal circumstances, such as your finances and home set-up.

We recognize that the challenges at any stage of your illness can sometimes leave you feeling confused and overwhelmed. Your self-confidence may plummet and you may be emotionally upset. Each of these reactions can, in turn, affect your ability to cope. We have written this book with you and your experiences in mind. It is designed to help you to cope better with your circumstances. We cannot hope to provide solutions to every problem that you encounter. However, with our extensive clinical and research experience, we will share with you a way to understand and cope better with some of the psychological effects of cancer.

A message of hope

This book is about living better with and getting on top of the emotionally challenging aspects of cancer. We aim to convey a message of hope that, even when confronted with life-challenging situations and health difficulties, you can approach your unique situation with greater confidence if you have appropriate knowledge, help and accessible social and professional support. This can alter the impact that illness has on you, physically and emotionally, and on your relationships. We believe that better support can improve health outcomes and arm you with strategies and techniques to improve your own coping.

The course, treatment and medical outcome of cancer may be something that you cannot directly control. You may find yourself relying on the input and intervention of medical specialists and other professionals. Coping with cancer is, however, as much about managing the psychological aspects: indeed, it is the psychological factors that you can more directly influence through how you choose to live with cancer.

While it is essential to trust in medical and nursing experts to monitor, advise, assess and treat the physical illness, managing your thoughts and feelings can improve your mental health. This, in turn, has been demonstrated to improve health outcomes in many situations. Your psychological response is something that you can work on to help your overall treatment, care and quality of life. This can be done on your own, in the context of family relationships and with the support of qualified professionals such as psychologists and counsellors. This book addresses how you can better understand and take charge of the way you cope psychologically.

The challenges

While it is true that we can never predict exactly how a person will respond to cancer, we have also seen that there are common challenges which people face. We have made these the focus of this book. We aim to provide a practical and helpful handbook for people coping with and adapting to the emotional challenges of living with cancer. Where we can, we will guide you to other sources that can help you with specific issues and problems not covered here.

Our approach is modern and upfront, just as it is when we meet with people face-to-face in counselling sessions. It is not of the 'tell-me-about-your-childhood' approach to coping where the focus would typically be on your past. Instead, we encourage you to think about the link between thoughts, behaviours and emotions and to make use of practical strategies to deal with daily challenges. We also try to avoid jargon, and to be direct and clear in our style. We hope that this will not be misconstrued as being 'simplistic'. The book is not prescriptive, telling you how to live your life. Neither is it a discussion about the difference in effectiveness between different medical treatments for cancer. As psychologists and researchers, we deliberately avoid giving medical advice which is always best provided by your doctor, specialist oncologist or nurse specialist.

Psychological support can help you to cope better with your disease. People who are diagnosed with cancer handle the challenges it presents in different ways. Many find that psychological counselling is as helpful for them as it is for their partner, family and loved ones. This may be particularly valuable at certain times – while undergoing tests, say – or in response to specific challenges, such as low mood, telling your children or coping with the physical changes you may experience.

Four key factors are important in adjusting to a cancer diagnosis and its psychological impact on you and your family:

1 good support from family and friends;
2 open communication between people about what is happening and what to prepare for;
3 managing illness, specific symptoms, effects of treatment, stress, worry and uncertainty in practical and effective ways; and
4 an open and supportive relationship with your oncologist and nurses.

Coping with the psychological effects of cancer does not mean having to cope on your own. Good coping means being open to the support of family members, friends, professional caregivers and those from voluntary organizations too.

We have included numerous case vignettes to illustrate the varied psychological effects of cancer and the unique experiences of people with whom we have worked. The cases are based on real circumstances but have been extensively disguised and re-worked so as to preserve their confidential nature.

This book is primarily about the psychological effects of cancer. Therefore, in Chapter 2 we reflect on the emotional impact of a cancer diagnosis. For some people, this can be quite extensive and unsettling. Fear, anger, envy, loss and grief, anxiety, depression, discouragement and loneliness may be experienced at some or many points after diagnosis.

Chapter 3 explains why illness has such a strong emotional component. Here, we reflect on the subtle interrelationship between our thoughts, our emotions and the way we act or behave. This chapter also considers the place that illness has in our lives – what *meaning* we give to it. Chapter 4 builds on this by introducing techniques that may help you to deal with distressing thoughts and feelings by providing constructive, everyday solutions to emotional problems.

Sometimes our reactions to challenging situations can inadvertently perpetuate emotional challenges. In Chapter 5 we discuss ways to understand the link between emotions and actions. We highlight ways to identify which behaviours may not be helpful and how to tackle them.

Many people with cancer experience significant stress and may feel emotionally overwhelmed. Chapter 6 focuses specifically on relaxation techniques which can help the way you think and feel. These are useful in many situations and may also help you to control the physical symptoms of stress, anxiety and worry.

Illness affects us not in isolation but in the context of those who are close to us emotionally. In Chapter 7, we explore how cancer can affect family relationships and the impact on family structure. Intimate personal relationships may also come under strain, and in Chapter 8 we discuss the effect that illness may have on couple relationships and on one's partner.

For some people with cancer, their illness may be terminal. In Chapter 9, we discuss issues that may arise for people in these circumstances. We consider the emotional impact of receiving bad news and how this may affect family and relationships.

Your relationship with healthcare professionals is extremely important too, and we explore this in Chapter 10. The chapter also provides practical information on managing the anxieties associated with your hospital or clinic visits.

The main focus of the book is the emotional and social effects of cancer. The clinical aspects of cancer and its treatment are extensively covered in other books such as *The Biology of Cancer* by Robert Weinberg (Garland Press, London, 2006), as well as in patient support websites. These aspects are also best addressed in the context of your clinical visits. See 'Useful addresses and finance' on p. 102 for a good starting point to a deeper understanding of cancer and its treatment. This section also includes website addresses we hope you may find useful, and a short section on finances.

Illness is never welcome and a diagnosis of cancer can be hard to bear. We hope that the ideas, information and psychological skills discussed in this book will help you and your loved ones to move forward with a life that is as fulfilled as it can be in spite of the challenges that you face.

2

The emotional impact of cancer

A diagnosis of cancer is the starting point for a number of issues that we discuss in this book. While there may have been unexplained symptoms beforehand, the diagnosis from a doctor is really the beginning of a person's 'relationship' with the illness. From this point onwards, life may need to change considerably: the medical aspects of the condition need to be managed, as do some of the psychological aspects, according to what is known about them. This time also marks the start of a 'relationship' with healthcare professionals and can alter patterns in family relationships (see Chapters 7 and 8).

A diagnosis of cancer may be the culmination of months of worry and perhaps several investigations into symptoms. It may come as a relief for some people to finally know what is wrong and to put an end to the uncertainty, while for others it may be completely unexpected. Whether or not the person is prepared for the diagnosis, it almost always comes as a huge shock for the individual as well as his or her loved ones.

Denial

Cancer can present in many different ways and with a variety of signs and symptoms. Some of these are transient, while some signs may be vague and non-specific. It's no wonder that we may not always recognize these and other signs as possibly indicating an underlying problem. Even when some symptoms are more obviously warning signs, it is normal first to avoid visiting the doctor or to deny that there may be something seriously wrong. Denial of illness is a first stage in adjusting to the possibility of 'bad news'. Perhaps our age, healthy lifestyle and absence of any previous history or serious illness leads us to discount the symptoms or elect to 'wait and see'.

There are other reasons why people may delay approaching their doctor, even when they have suspicions that something more worrying is going on. We may be fearful of what might follow from a visit to the surgery, or that some symptoms are embarrassing and difficult to talk about. Others feel anxious being in a clinic or hospital. These concerns are real and they are very common. Of course, denial is normal and everyone does this at some time in order to avoid possible unpleasant consequences. Avoiding something because we are afraid of it is a natural survival instinct. When it comes to cancer and other health problems, however, denying the possibility that we might be ill can have negative consequences, particularly if it means delaying treatment. Many cancers are better managed if they are diagnosed early and if treatment begins before they advance.

Fears associated with illness can be allayed by gaining insight into our condition and by getting appropriate professional help, support and treatment. This starts with a visit to the doctor. Aric suspected that something might be wrong, but it was not easy to approach his doctor and he was worried about what he might find out about his health:

Aric's persistent urge to urinate troubled him. When he began to feel pain when passing urine, his worries intensified. Embarrassed by his symptoms, he first tried to self-diagnose himself over the internet, hoping to avoid a visit to the doctor. He became more concerned when he learned that his symptoms might indicate problems with his prostate. His anxiety levels increased, along with his physical symptoms, and he started having trouble sleeping and began to lose weight. He was convinced that he had cancer and would need invasive and painful treatment that would have some unpleasant and lasting side-effects. Fear of further investigations and of the possible diagnosis kept him away from his doctor for many months until his symptoms were unbearable and began to severely affect his day-to-day life.

He finally presented to his GP with symptoms of severe pain on urination as well as with extreme anxiety. His GP took some urine and blood samples and performed a rectal examination. This is what Aric had been dreading, but his doctor was reassuring and put him at ease. He was able to view it as part of the diagnosis and treatment process for his symptoms. On his referral to hospital for further testing and biopsy, he was surprised to find himself in an environment where the staff were caring, knowledgeable and experienced. They were professional and objective about the symptoms he had found embarrassing, because they had treated many patients like him.

The way we cope with illness

All kinds of people are diagnosed with cancer and not everyone is affected in the same way. Your personality plays a part in how you respond to your diagnosis and to being ill in general. Past experience is important too. Having coped with adverse life events in the past may arm some with the experience and skills they need to manage the shock of diagnosis. People who are typically stoical or 'thick-skinned' may fare better than those who are more passive and who feel that they have less control over their lives. Others who cope well in the face of adversity may find these innate skills useful when faced with illness.

Some people may find the sudden focus on them and their own needs difficult. Others do well when they are the centre of attention and feel cared for. A few draft in everyone they can think of to help, while others prefer to cope alone or may be over-sensitive about burdening others. It's easy to see how these underlying personality styles play a part in people's experiences of coping with cancer.

There are other personal and situational factors that affect how we cope with illness, including personal history with cancer, the type of cancer, its location in the body and type of treatments. While we cannot predict exactly how a person is going to be affected, it is reasonable to say that many will experience emotional challenges alongside their physical ones. This is often a certainty in the face of serious and life-threatening illnesses, particularly when they are unexpected. Most people cope with and adjust to these challenges well, but for some, negative feelings persist and can develop into more serious emotional problems, such as depression.

Chronic illness and cure

Chronic illnesses are not rare. About one in three people in the UK have a chronic condition of some kind and some people have more than one. Advances in medicine mean that illnesses that may have led to death in the past are no longer fatal. Many people are living with their conditions, and this includes cancer.

The term 'cancer' actually covers more than 200 different medical conditions, each with its own name, symptoms, diagnostic tests and treatment, but with some features in common. All cancers arise because certain cells in the body develop problems in the way they grow and behave. There are a number of reasons why this might happen and the symptoms of cancer generally arise because tumours interfere with normal body functions.

In the UK, the most common cancers that affect people are breast cancer, prostate cancer, lung cancer and bowel cancer – there were an estimated two million cases of cancer in the UK in 2008. To put it another way, one in 30 people in the UK have some form of cancer, most commonly breast, bowel or prostate (source: Cancer Research UK).

What are chronic illnesses?

While a chronic health condition need not be life-threatening, most will be life-challenging. Often there is no obvious, identifiable cause and the illness may develop over a long period of time. There may be a history of troubling, unexplained symptoms before doctors are able to diagnose the underlying condition. People must usually adapt their lives to accommodate changes in their ability, or to fit in their treatment and its consequences. It is a fact that some people will die from their disease.

All these features set chronic conditions apart from the acute ones (like bronchitis) which tend to start more quickly, usually have an identifiable cause (e.g. bronchitis is caused by bacteria or viruses) and are 'self-limiting'. This means they usually run their course and are then over. Another key difference is that many acute illnesses respond well to treatments and are 'cured'. Chronic illnesses, on the other hand, don't usually go away. Cancer is one such chronic condition where the idea of a 'cure' as a single fix that will get rid of the disease may not always be applicable, although the rapid advances in this speciality make this an ever more likely possibility. If caught early enough, some cancers can be treated effectively and may never return. With some types of cancer, long remissions, where the condition lies dormant, are not uncommon.

With some forms of cancer, sadly, the opposite may also occur. There may be few or no signs of advancing disease, which may only be diagnosed at an advanced stage where it is untreatable.

Many people with chronic illnesses experience a worsening of their symptoms over time, often despite the treatment they receive. People with such progressive conditions must live with the knowledge that their symptoms will worsen and, if they are terminally ill, that they will probably die from their disease. Many cancers are progressive, particularly advanced cancers that have spread from their original site and lead to tumours in other parts of the body.

What will be the outcome?

Advances in medicine mean that many people achieve remission and live for years without recurrence. Indeed, an increasing number may make a full recovery and lead a full and normal life. For certain cancer types, as well as advanced cancers, the outlook may be less favourable and the treatments will be palliative, i.e. with a view to improving quality of life by preventing life-threatening symptoms or easing troublesome ones.

Your prognosis depends on the type of cancer you have and the stage at which you receive treatment. Some cancers, such as lung cancer, are more difficult to treat and the outlook is generally poor. Whatever your medical prognosis, to learn you have cancer can be devastating. Naturally, you will wonder whether you will be cured or whether your outcome will be less positive. People who are diagnosed with terminal cancer may face particular challenges; we address these in Chapter 9.

Phases of illness from an emotional perspective

Some health professionals find it helpful to think of chronic illnesses as having distinct phases or stages, with the diagnosis as a starting point. The stages are by no means fixed, and they will have different meanings and will manifest in different ways for different people.

People often experience a 'crisis' phase around the time of their diagnosis, which is usually associated with intense emotions. You may feel frightened and at a loss, and struggle to take the implications on board. Many people are literally in shock after receiving bad news, feeling emotionally numb and unable to take in anything else during that consultation with their doctor. This is a time of emotional vulnerability and you will need to quickly mobilize support and begin to learn how to manage what you are feeling. Alongside these challenges are the physical symptoms of the illness and decisions about treatments.

This phase is often characterized by acute distress as the reality of ill health sets in, and you may feel emotionally unsettled for many weeks, maybe experiencing anger or self-blame. Often there is nothing or no-one to blame, yet the shock and anger persist, without any target or helpful explanation for the cause of illness. There will be much to learn and to come to grips with.

Your family and loved ones may be in emotional turmoil too, trying to adjust in their own ways to the news of your illness. They may be as bewildered and anxious as you and on a similar emotional rollercoaster. They may also need to mobilize themselves to offer support and take care of you. Your whole social and family network may be going through much of what you are experiencing. Some may rally and be supportive; others may mean well but upset you with their ideas and suggestions; still others may simply disappear, finding it all too much to bear emotionally.

A 'stabilization' period may follow the early crisis phase. This may be a time of adjustment to your cancer, where you are learning first-hand how it will affect you. It is a time of enquiry and adaptation. You may gain a better sense of how your life is changing and how to accommodate the restrictions that your condition is placing on you. These adjustments may make this a difficult time. Relationships with loved ones may need to adapt; roles within the family often shift. Depending on your diagnosis and treatment regime, you may need to come to terms with stopping work for a period or changing some other aspects of your lifestyle.

In the 'resolution' phase that follows, people may come to a kind of 'peace' with their situation and their illness. This phase is characterized by settling into a different version of life and a return to some definition of 'ordinariness'. You may feel a degree of acceptance of what your condition means to you medically, spiritually and emotionally. The upheaval and painful challenges to your identity may level off. Having a good support network and receiving appropriate medical management can greatly assist this. By this stage, you may feel that your illness no longer dominates all aspects of your life. This doesn't mean that you are 'happy' being ill, but rather that you have come to accommodate illness in your life, finding a place for it, while also putting it in its place by not letting it affect everything you do or feel.

Some of the descriptions or phases above may seem unrealistic or too clear-cut, but the phases of illness are not fixed and neither are the definitions of them. It is better to think of them as circular, rather than as a line that starts with crisis and ends with resolution. People move between phases as their circumstances change. This is entirely normal; it is harder to adjust to some losses than others and there will be easier times and more difficult ones.

> When Mohammed attended his 18-month follow-up examination, he was told that the cancer had come back and he would need further treatment. Fortunately, the recurrence was local and detected at a very early stage, which meant that it might still be treatable. The recurrence brought back many of the same emotions that Mohammed felt when he was first diagnosed with cancer. He initially felt shocked and became increasingly angry with the medical team for not having managed to stop the cancer the first time. He was also angry with himself for going through the previous course of treatment, feeling that it had made no difference.
>
> Mohammed became increasingly anxious about the prospect of enduring another course of treatment. He was losing hope and became doubtful that his cancer could ever be cured. He wanted to appear strong and calm, thinking that he had put his family through enough grief the first time around. For the next couple of weeks, he continued to suppress his fears and worries, becoming increasingly overwhelmed by the day. It was his wife, Nita, who finally persuaded Mohammed to talk about his emotions. With her help, Mohammed was able to confront his experience of anxiety and despair. Mohammed's second cancer treatment went well and he continues to attend the hospital for follow-up checks.

Some people with cancer as well as professionals don't find words like 'acceptance' and 'denial' very helpful, feeling that this detracts from the real ups and downs associated with adjusting to illness.

This sort of language may suggest an element of shortcoming in people who are 'denying' illness, rather than 'accepting' it. We have found that words that give an idea of difference or range may be more helpful to describe these times and emotions, such as 'unsettled' and 'settled', 'extraordinary' and 'ordinary', 'harmony' and 'disharmony', for example. The purpose of trying to find better ways to describe these phases and accompanying feelings is really to acknowledge that illness has an impact on people and that this extends beyond the physical effects.

For the remainder of this chapter we talk about some of the emotions that you may experience. These are normal though sometimes unwelcome responses to life-changing events. Not everyone who has cancer will experience these challenges to the degree that they feel professional help is needed to cope with them. Certain problems may subside over time, particularly if the prognosis is good.

Some psychologists have suggested six main hurdles that people with cancer might face. These are a useful way of thinking about the nature of challenges you may face:

- managing uncertainty;
- searching for meaning;
- dealing with loss of control;
- having a need for openness in relationships;
- having a need for emotional support;
- having a need for medical support.[1]

The majority of people with cancer adjust to these challenges on their own and there are also ways to enhance coping (see Chapters 4, 5 and 6), but up to a fifth of people with cancer may develop emotional problems that require professional help, sometimes only realizing the lasting negative emotional effects of surviving cancer after their medical treatment is over. This is where professionals such as psychologists and counsellors can help.

Fear

It is not surprising that a diagnosis of cancer is often clouded with fear and dread. Having cancer may force us to face up to some difficult questions, many of which we may not be able to answer.

What impact will illness have on our life? How will we balance the demands of our condition with those of being a parent, or a partner? Will our work suffer? Do we fully understand what we are being told? Will we die? The facts about our illness – even if they are unpleasant and frightening in themselves – will at least be a firm foundation for coping. Reliable information is very important. Much of what we hear about cancer may reflect what is at one extreme end of experience. However, remember that cancer is common. Millions of people worldwide are dealing with it.

Anxiety is often linked to uncertainty. Cancer patients often experience anxiety: at the time of diagnosis, when presenting for further investigations, while waiting to hear about test results, and after receiving treatment. This is a natural and expected response. Indeed, it is unusual for people not to experience some degree of hesitancy, concern or worry when faced with these experiences. However, just as prolonged and severe sadness may be indicative of underlying depression, prolonged and severe anxiety may indicate that you are having a problem adjusting to the uncertainty around your illness. Severe anxieties can manifest as phobias, e.g. claustrophobia, or an extreme anxiety associated with needles. These may interfere with assessment or treatment regimens such as when needing to undergo a CAT or MRI scan or during chemotherapy or routine blood tests. A psychologist or counsellor can help to treat these and related symptoms of anxiety. For anxiety disorders, targeted psychological and drug treatments can be very effective.

An underlying fear about your health may always be there. You may be afraid of what the future holds, or of your cancer returning. If your illness is terminal, alongside the other emotions associated with serious illness, you may be confronted with the fear of dying. Whatever the nature of your fears, these are bound to be normal and ones that your doctors and nurses have helped people with before.

Cancer patients commonly report a number of fears, which include:

- pain;
- loss of a future;
- loss of physical or mental ability;

- disfigurement (from illness or treatment);
- stigma;
- death.

Avoidance is a perfectly normal way of coping with fear. However, fear can prevent you from doing things that you are capable of doing, things which could improve your quality of life. A person undergoing chemotherapy, for example, may avoid leaving the house for fear of how people will respond to his or her hair loss, or someone experiencing pain may worry excessively about situations that could make the pain feel worse. In a paradoxical way, avoidance tends to make people more fearful and less confident and therefore less able to manage their fears.

Fear is a natural response to an unwelcome and potentially life-threatening event and should be accepted as such. It is not easy to challenge or confront the things that we are afraid of, but the goal is not to let fear dominate our lives. If we let it, it can have a negative impact on our quality of life, our relationships and our wellbeing. There are constructive ways to tackle fear, including seeking information, restructuring negative thoughts and emotions, solving problems and trying not to avoid exposure to certain situations. A starting point is to list the things that we fear and then to talk to people we trust about these. There are practical responses to nearly everything we fear, and trying them can improve confidence and coping. If you feel overwhelmed by your fears or are having difficulty responding to them in a way that improves your coping, this is surely the time to consult with a psychologist or counsellor.

Anger and envy

Anger is a normal response to loss and a part of many well-documented cycles of adjustment to illness. You may have every reason to be angry with a doctor for failing to diagnose your illness earlier. Anger and frustration can also stem from feeling overwhelmed with tiredness or overburdened with managing your condition, or simply from feeling that the situation is unfair. 'Why me?' you might ask, and 'Why now?' Self-reproach may be one response. You may feel that some of your own actions have worsened your condition or even caused it. You may be angry at yourself for not having sought treatment sooner.

Anger can be both positive and negative. We may put it to good use by turning it into being assertive and strong but when it goes unchecked and unaddressed there can be a host of problems, both for ourselves and for the people around us. *It can affect our physical health, mood and relationships, as well as how much we take care of ourselves. These can all impact negatively on the course of our illness. Anger can and should be managed.* Approaches include developing assertiveness skills, learning how to solve problems rather than blaming ourselves or others, finding more useful outlets for emotional expression, learning to 'walk away' from it and giving ourselves space and time to relax (see p. 48).

Envy can also be a response to changes and losses that occur during our adjustment to cancer. You may be envious of apparently healthy people: is it fair that you are ill while they are healthy? Do they value what they have or do they take their health for granted? People who need to change their working patterns or give up work may envy their colleagues. Any financial pressures that result may heighten these feelings.

Feeling discouraged

Lifestyle changes and cancer treatment regimens may become wearing, particularly when nothing seems to make a difference to how you are feeling. Competing needs may give rise to discouragement and frustration. While you attempt to meet some aspects of these needs, others may be neglected.

These are just some of the things that can lead to feeling discouraged and disillusioned:

- ongoing pain;
- sleep problems and cumulative fatigue;
- side-effects of medications;
- difficulties focusing or concentrating;
- problems with sex drive or ability to enjoy sex.

Tiredness can be both a symptom of cancer and a side-effect of treatment. Physical exhaustion can make day-to-day life or more demanding hurdles seem mountainous.

Depression and low mood

Depression can affect anyone at any age and in any state of physical health. About half of the total number of people with cancer will have some of the symptoms of depression (see below) but an actual depressive illness is less common (about one in four).

It is important to make a distinction between depression and depressed mood (or sadness). Sadness is often an expected part of adjusting to cancer but may not be constant. The problem is when these feelings are severe and prolonged. Symptoms vary, but usually depression or low mood manifests as:

- tiredness;
- low motivation;
- a desire to give up on normal activities;
- sleep problems (too much sleep, interrupted sleep or inability to get to sleep);
- loss of appetite (or overeating);
- sighing a lot;
- not wanting to spend time with people; withdrawing socially;
- reduced sexual interest;
- low self-confidence;
- feelings of worthlessness.

The relationship between cancer and depression is not straightforward. Depression may stem from having cancer and an inability to adjust to illness, or could be a side-effect of treatment. For some, it may even have little to do with cancer, being linked to another life event such as bereavement or a marital problem.

Symptoms of depression can interfere with treatment and with self-care. Depression can also increase your susceptibility to other health problems and to drinking, smoking, lethargy (not taking exercise) and overeating. Early recognition and treatment of low mood can prevent more severe symptoms and reduce the impact on your illness and general wellbeing.

Loneliness

There is a difference between loneliness and being alone, although the two can be linked. We all know that we can feel lonely even when surrounded by people. For some people, cancer will mean that they are alone less often than they used to be, because of regular clinic or hospital visits or because friends and loved ones have rallied round. It is still possible to feel alienated and lonely, though. Loneliness is often associated with feeling excluded from a group. In spite of best intentions, you may feel that your well-meaning friends don't truly understand the challenges you are facing and that their lives are insurmountably different from your own.

Cancer can be isolating. People affected may experience prejudice from their colleagues, family or even insurance companies. Signs of illness or its treatment such as hair loss from chemotherapy or scars from surgery may be noticed by friends or strangers, causing us to feel isolated and stigmatized. The social aspects of illness can at times be more distressing than the physical ones.

Family and friends may withdraw. They may be afraid, embarrassed or confused. If they don't literally stop visiting, they may refuse to acknowledge the seriousness of your challenges, leaving you feeling rejected and isolated. Cancer can impact on your social or professional life, leaving you housebound and isolated. There can be problems in relationships too, particularly if treatment has changed your body and the way you feel about yourself. Amanda's experience illustrates this.

> Amanda's breast cancer was first picked up during a routine screening examination when she was 57 years old. She was a healthy, active, middle-aged woman, in a happy and stable relationship for 13 years with her second husband. Investigations revealed that her cancer had not spread beyond her breast and she was advised to have a mastectomy. The news was devastating for her. She recovered physically from the operation but found it more difficult to adjust to the way her body looked after the surgery. Her scars and missing breast were a constant reminder of her illness and she felt that her husband's feelings towards her had changed. She noticed how difficult he found it to touch her in the ways he used to and this reinforced her feelings of being less attractive to him. These reactions affected her self-esteem, and while she and her husband had enjoyed a healthy sex life prior to her diagnosis there were many difficulties after her surgery. Amanda was able to talk about some of her concerns with her nurse specialist, who suggested that she and her husband attend a few counselling sessions with a couples therapist. Here they found a forum in which they could discuss

sensitive concerns and get practical advice from an objective person. They were able to discuss their concerns as a couple. Amanda learned that she was not on her own with anxieties about the effects of her surgery. Her husband was able to tell her how he worried about hurting her emotionally. By opening up communication between them about sensitive issues, the couple learned to adjust to their new circumstances and to provide mutual care and support. Their sex life improved after the counselling sessions.

Loss and grieving

Illness inevitably means changes in our way of life, such as in routines, in our ability to do things, in our emotions and maybe even in relationships with family and friends. We grieve when we lose things that we are used to having and when we lose the things we rely on to be who we are. Feeling that we have lost control of the situation can have an impact on our self-esteem and may leave us feeling powerless.

There are a number of other losses commonly associated with cancer:

- loss of income;
- loss of enjoyment;
- loss of freedom and independence;
- losing your 'old self';
- reduced levels of confidence;
- loss of skills or abilities;
- loss of hope;
- loss of control over situations or over your body;
- an end to 'normal' relationships;
- loss of specific functions such as mobility, sexual performance, clear vision, clear thinking;
- a change in your appearance, such as hair loss, weight gain or loss, scars and, in some cases, having to have parts of your body removed.

Feelings of worthlessness

Many of us measure our worth and the worth of others by achievements. When illness forces changes in these or other areas that define us, we may begin to feel worthless. Parents may find that having to adapt or withdraw from their supportive and protective role in a family is a particularly heavy burden and one that challenges their sense of 'worth'. Associated with this may be feelings of guilt for exposing our children to difficulties. Illness has an impact on capability, which in turn affects our identity and sense of worth.

We have highlighted some of the emotional challenges that can affect you. In spite of their being unwelcome, we have also tried to emphasize that many of them can be managed and overcome. Some are temporary, while others may require more vigorous intervention. Whatever your reactions, you should never feel alone in having to deal with them. Your family and loved ones, as well as professional caregivers, are a vital source of support. Don't be surprised, however, if there are times when even apparently minor events or situations make you feel vulnerable or sad. This is normal and expected. We now go on to focus on skills and strategies you can use to prevent some challenging feelings from dominating your life with cancer.

3

Regaining control

While cancer may 'programme' fairly predictable physical symptoms and health problems, the psychological responses are not pre-programmed. There is an enormous range in people's emotional responses. This impact isn't always linked to the severity of the condition, and people with the same diagnosis may respond very differently from one another. Of more importance is the *meaning* that the illness has in a person's life and how he or she can therefore *cope* with it.

We all experience illness in a context that is unique and we will each assign unique meanings to being ill. This meaning frames our approach to managing disease as well as how we interact with loved ones and healthcare providers.

With a clear understanding of your health beliefs, you will find it easier to do something about any negative ones and to enhance those that contribute positively to how you are coping. 'Coping' does not mean an absence of emotional distress. It means that the distress does not necessarily continually overwhelm you, even though there may be times when it may feel overwhelming. Some people describe having cancer as an 'opportunity' to get close to other people and to assign priorities in their lives. In this sense, illness can be a 'mixed blessing' which has forced a reassessment of one's goals, relationships and values.

Impact on beliefs

Any illness, but particularly life-threatening and terminal conditions, can affect our beliefs. We may begin to question beliefs we thought were fundamental to our identity and to re-evaluate basic ideas we have about living, and indeed about dying. Your determined view on why we are here and the purpose of your life may be shaken by a contemplation of your own mortality. Some

21

people look for spiritual help in their search for understanding and meaning. People may find solace in learning about approaches that they might never have considered before. Some may question or even renounce their religion in the face of their own illness or the illness of someone close to them.

The impact on beliefs can also be more subtle. Your confidence and certainty about your role as a parent is disrupted by the changes you are going through. A dedicated career person who has always worked hard to be successful and wealthy may question the purpose of these achievements in the face of illness. In the most direct way, illness can change what we believe in and what we believe about ourselves. The independent, brave, stalwart character you thought you would always be may be elusive when you are ill, or may come and go alongside the changes in your symptoms.

Research suggests that those who are able to acknowledge and express their feelings seem to adjust better to illness, and in some cases have better health outcomes. There is much more to coping with illness than simply recognizing and treating physical symptoms. Health beliefs play a large part in the way we respond mentally, emotionally and spiritually to illness. These result from a complex interaction of factors, including our:

- background;
- experiences;
- personality;
- family;
- culture;
- religion (if we follow one).

The above factors help shape our attitudes towards illness. Given the range of our exposure to different events, people, opinions, etc., it is not surprising that some will contribute negatively to how we think and behave. You may have come across or cared for a close family member with cancer in the past and your fears about your own condition could be bound up with your experiences of this. Our attitudes towards illness and health care all have their origin somewhere, and you may find it helpful to reflect on what may have contributed to yours. This will help you to define what you believe in, and also to identify any negative views – aside from the expected ones – about being ill.

Beliefs can be as firmly established in our thinking as old habits are in our behaviour. Identifying these before they become 'mental traps' is a starting point in trying to tackle them. We should always remember that beliefs are not fixed: they can change in response to new information and experiences or as we mature. Your emotional response to your illness needn't be fixed or predictable. It can change, and sometimes you may need to do certain things in order to change it. This is the basis of many of the chapters in this book.

'Constraining beliefs', such as thinking you are directly responsible for your illness, can impact negatively on how you cope. You may give up, either literally or in your mind, and feel defeated by your condition. Other attitudes, such as believing that you do not deserve to be ill and that you are resilient and resourceful, or that your faith and support from your loved ones will help you, can be enhancing ones. The challenge is to try and change constraining beliefs into enhancing ones. A good place to start is to define your views and reflect upon what has shaped them. Consider the following questions, either on your own or in conversation with a close friend or counsellor:

- What *views* do your family hold about *modern medicine in general*? What are your views? Is there a conflict between your views and those of family members?
- Do your family or close friends have particular *views or attitudes towards you* and *your illness*? Do they express these?
- Is there any *stigma or shame* associated with your condition? Do you find that people respond in a particular way to your illness when they hear about it for the first time? How do you respond to these reactions? Is your illness or the consequences of it obvious when people look at you? How would you like them to react? How might you react in their positions?
- What do you believe *caused* your illness? Emotions such as guilt and helplessness will affect what you believe modern medicine can do for you and how you care for yourself.
- What *hopes* do you have about doctors and about the modern

treatments that you are receiving or that might be prescribed in future?

- Do you believe that you are getting the *best information and care* available to you? Are there other things that you feel are missing?

- Has a *previous experience* with cancer affected the way you cope with a recent diagnosis? You may have learned some coping skills from someone close to you. Identifying and developing these skills will help you to cope with your own challenges.

- Have you *told people* that you have cancer? Or do you want to keep it *private*? Do you find it difficult to tell people that something is wrong medically? Do you find it easier to tell some people and not others? Are there people you would like to tell but haven't? Do you think you might tell them at another time?

These questions may not have been easy or straightforward to answer. However, through considering what you believe about having cancer, you may discover that you hold certain helpful

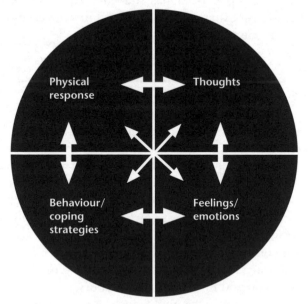

Figure 3.1 The 'hot cross bun' model

or unhelpful views. These may have an effect on how you understand cancer, what you think your treatment can do for you and the strength of your relationships with loved ones, as well as with doctors and your approaches to self-care.

To understand why people respond differently to a diagnosis of cancer, it is important to recognize that there is a link between what we feel, what we think and how we act. People have different coping styles, but those who seem to cope better have been found to have better health outcomes. If you feel that you're not coping well, it may be helpful to address the underlying 'cause' of a particular emotion or behaviour that may be having a negative effect, either on your own or with a psychologist or a counsellor. Such enquiry and reflection and changes in how we act are the basis for cognitive behavioural therapy, which is an approach to treating emotional problems. The focus is on how our cognitive processes (thoughts, beliefs, attitudes) affect our behaviour (and hence the way we cope with illness). The diagram in Figure 3.1 – called the 'hot cross bun' model – shows that these four dimensions are linked to one another.

The idea is that it is not the *situations* themselves that cause the emotional distress, but instead how we *think* about them. There may be a range of interrelated responses to something which happens to us, including a feeling in relation to the experience, thoughts and images in response to it, and physical changes such as muscle tension or rapid breathing as well as other reactions or behavioural responses. Together, these dimensions make up our coping response. In Lisa's story, we have highlighted specific examples of thoughts and behaviours to illustrate how you can interpret these aspects for yourself.

Lisa, aged 28, had been diagnosed with cervical cancer following a routine cervical smear test at her local hospital. She felt nervous about sharing the news with her family, especially her mother because they were so close (*emotion*). Lisa was convinced she would cause her mother to become upset and worried once she found out about the cancer (*thought or belief*). She pictured her mother sitting on the sofa crying inconsolably for hours on end, just as she had done when Lisa's grandmother suffered a heart attack five years earlier (*negative image*). When she visited her mother, Lisa pretended she was fine and avoided any mention of illness or health-related issues (*behaviour*). She could feel her heart racing (*physical symptom*) every time her mother talked about a neighbour who had fallen ill or an old colleague who had suffered a recent loss of a loved one. She felt increasingly guilty about hiding the news from her mother (*emotion*) and decided to tell her during a weekend break in the countryside. While her mother was initially upset (*emotion/reaction*), Lisa was surprised at how confidently and supportively she acted during the rest of the weekend (*reinterpretation*). Lisa felt immediate relief and her anxiety level rapidly decreased (*positive emotions and behaviours or reactions*).This made her realize that her mother was much stronger than Lisa had initially anticipated she would be (*re-appraisal or new belief*).

Identifying your thoughts gives you an opportunity to challenge any 'faulty' thinking that may be underpinning your emotional reaction. A deeper understanding of these responses, as illustrated above, will enable you to develop alternative ways of interpreting challenging situations. Lisa felt nervous about sharing her concerns with her family. In particular, she didn't want to add to her mother's worries. Her attempts to hide her diagnosis had an unpleasant physical effect on her as well as reinforcing negative feelings. Once Lisa was able to tell her mother about her illness and witnessed her reacting supportively and confidently, she was able to reinterpret her situation and change the assumptions she had made about her mother's behaviour.

While thoughts play an important part in the way people cope with cancer, we are not advocating a simplistic 'positive thinking' approach, an approach that can victimize people, making them feel that somehow their sadness, fears, anger or hopelessness are unacceptable and may even be responsible for their condition. Undeniably, coping will be more difficult if negative emotions persist. These can affect our self-esteem and our confidence, lower our mood and make us feel vulnerable and depressed. Psychologists have identified a number of common thinking patterns that perpetuate negative emotions:[1]

1 *All-or-nothing thinking*: a tendency to think in absolute or extreme terms about a situation, usually in a negative way. For example, you may think at the time of diagnosis: 'My cancer

can't be cured' or 'I am going to die', when this needn't necessarily be the case.

2 *Over-generalization*: a tendency to use individual experiences as
evidence that something (usually negative) will happen all the
time (a false rule). For example, you may think that because you
have cancer you will never be free from other serious illness in
the future (i.e. a stroke or heart problems), although the fact is
that many people who recover from cancer are at no greater risk
of these conditions.

3 *Mental filter*: focusing on negative or upsetting experiences or
thoughts while ignoring other aspects that paint a different
picture of the situation. For example, you may think: 'My treatment is not going to work' ignoring the important fact that
there are a variety of different treatments and no two people
respond in the same way.

4 *Disqualifying the positive*: discounting positive experiences
because it is difficult to replace strongly held pessimistic views
or memories. For example: 'Even though the doctors are optimistic about my recovery, there is always a chance that they
may be wrong.'

5 *Jumping to conclusions or mind-reading*: a tendency to assume
that the worst will happen in spite of a lack of evidence. For
example, when attending your sister's wedding shortly after
treatment, you may feel worried that you will not be able to
enjoy the event. You may worry that your sister will be very
disappointed in this, when in fact she is delighted and grateful
that you are able to be there with the rest of the family.

6 *Catastrophizing*: exaggeration of negative characteristics of a
person or situation, however unlikely they are. For example,
you might think that the delay in your test results means bad
news, that your treatment is not working and the doctors are
trying to find a way to tell you 'the worst'.

7 *Emotional reasoning*: making decisions according to how you
feel rather than on the facts. For example: 'I feel very anxious.
My heart is pounding and I feel faint. Something bad is going
to happen to me, I just know it.'

8 *Should, must and have to*: having thoughts that are somehow
distorted and tending to be 'fixed' rigidly into a response or

situation. This may be governed by quite extreme or inflexible rules. For example, you might feel that you should be able to cope with what is happening and that you shouldn't have any negative feelings because these indicate emotional weakness.

9 *Labelling*: similar to over-generalization, reflecting a tendency to explain events through categorizing, labelling or naming them in fixed terms, rather than by describing them behaviourally. For example: 'The hospital was full of frightened patients', rather than 'Some patients got worried when a computer glitch meant they had to re-arrange their medical appointments.'

10 *Personalization or attribution*: exaggerating causation when facts do not necessarily support this. For example: 'I got up and felt dizzy; it must have been because I overdid things yesterday', when in fact dizziness is a known side-effect of some medications.

Make a note of your own thoughts, then read through these thinking errors once more and see whether you can recognize any of them in your own reactions. By changing the way you think, you may reduce the intensity of your emotions. You will learn more about this in Chapter 4.

Dealing with other people's reactions

People around you will react differently to your illness. Even close friends may find it hard to know what to say. Instead, they may avoid seeing you, or avoid the topic of your cancer if they do. This can be very upsetting. You may choose to ignore any comments that upset you, or you may prefer to set the record straight where you can, explaining the reality at least of your own situation. The majority of your friends and colleagues will surely be well-meaning, but not all will fully understand what you are experiencing unless they themselves have had cancer.

What Can I Do to Help?[2] by Deborah Hutton is an excellent practical guide for friends and family about which behaviours are helpful and which aren't. Deborah's book was published in aid of Macmillan Cancer Support and draws on her own experiences to provide helpful advice:

- what to do in the difficult time immediately after you receive your diagnosis;
- what to do as a friend or family member;
- how to help during treatment;
- where to get more information;
- how to be helpful when the going gets tough.

4

Coping with distressing thoughts and feelings

In Chapter 2, we discussed typical emotional challenges following a diagnosis of cancer. No-one's future is certain, but when illness is a factor the unpredictability can make you feel frightened and at times overwhelmed. You may have experienced changes in your body and have lost some independence, and you may have had to make some significant changes to your daily life. These are very real changes or losses that are likely to affect you and those people close to you. Some people may sadly learn that their illness is terminal. If this is the case, some of the ideas described in Chapter 9 may be especially relevant for you. Everyone will respond in their own way to living with cancer, many feeling shock and anger and overwhelming sadness. These are understandable feelings, but for some people they can present considerable obstacles.

We describe a number of techniques in this chapter to help you cope with worry and negative thoughts. The approaches may be particularly relevant if your response to your illness, treatment and the future is dominated by intense anxiety.

Our expectations can greatly affect our reactions to life changes. What we say and do in a given situation is largely dependent on how we understand what is happening around us. Some people can be more distressed by their interpretation of events – such as over-focusing on things that might go wrong or on 'worst case scenarios' – than the actual event itself.

As we discussed in Chapter 3, the idea that our thinking is linked to our actions and our feelings is the fundamental principle of cognitive behavioural therapy. By understanding your thoughts and how they affect your emotions and behaviours, it is possible to develop alternative ways of interpreting worry and catastrophic thoughts. The exercises in this chapter may help you to recognize your negative thoughts and persistent worries. They may also help you to avoid bad thinking patterns. People who cope well in the face of cancer may already be approaching some of their own hurdles in these ways. Some of these approaches are a foundation for the interventions that people receive in counselling and therapy sessions. Psychologists and counsellors working within a cognitive behavioural therapy framework may promote some of these as ways to change negative thoughts or to help you better understand and gain control over your feelings. As with any new skills, learning them may require you to change or break old habits and commit yourself to a new course of action.

Understanding what you feel

A first step is to identify your dominant feelings. This is particularly important if they are negative emotions because of the effects they may be having on your behaviour and coping in general. Sometimes we do whatever we can to suppress negative emotions, perhaps because they feel overwhelming or because we do not have the skills to cope with them. We may also feel ashamed or guilty about what we feel. One positive way to cope with illness is to acknowledge and deal with emotions, rather than suppressing them. By doing something early on about our distress, we may avoid persistent and long-lasting negative feelings. Bottling up our fears and concerns may mean we are more likely to experience episodes of anxiety and depression. This happened to Jan.

> Jan was 50 years old when she was diagnosed with breast cancer following a routine breast-screening appointment. She was shocked and upset when her doctor told her the news. Her immediate worries were about her family, and she convinced herself that she needed to stay strong for the sake of her two daughters. Jan rarely spoke about her illness even though she felt frightened, angry and sad. When pressed to talk about how she was feeling or how she was coping, she brushed these questions aside. After having breast surgery, Jan declined the offer of counselling, even though her treatment affected her deeply and she felt anxious about the future and upset about the changes to her body.

She pushed a lot of her problems to the back of her mind and tried to maintain a positive and upbeat outlook. When her treatment was over, Jan was physically and emotionally exhausted and she gradually fell into a depression. She became inactive and withdrew from her friends and family. She no longer felt able to wear her brave face, even for her family. During a check-up visit to the hospital, her nurse noticed that Jan was not at all her usual self. She advised Jan to talk to a psychologist who could help her deal with the emotional effects of cancer.

Healthy emotions are an important part of our wellbeing. If you are not used to talking about the way you feel, it may be difficult to find words that truly reflect what you are going through. You may not realize that a particular emotion is persistent, or that you are experiencing it to a relatively extreme degree.

Keeping a daily diary of your dominant feelings can help you to reflect on emotions in a regular and systematic way. The following questions may help:

- What feeling is dominating right now?
- What mental images are associated with this feeling?
- When did I start feeling like this?
- Have I felt this before, and if so, when and where?
- How often do I feel this particular emotion?
- Am I doing anything to cope with my feelings? Is it helping or making the feeling worse?
- If I had a friend who was experiencing what I am right now, what could I say to make her or him feel better?

Other people can provide you with an outlet for your feelings. Consider talking to someone you trust – a close friend or a partner, perhaps – about what is troubling you. If you find it is too difficult to involve people you know well, consider a psychologist or counsellor. Remember that even if others cannot solve your medical or practical problems, they can at least listen to your experience. Cancer support groups provide another forum in which people can share their individual experiences and learn from those of others. Ask your doctor or nurse for contact details about support groups near you, or see 'Useful addresses and finance', p. 102.

Identify negative thoughts

As we have already seen, not all our thoughts are helpful ones, so it is a good idea to try to identify those that are negative. Look at your own ideas about cancer and its effect on you, your family and friends. Are these ideas constructive or unhelpful? Are they likely to help you cope with your illness or are they actually making you feel worse? Defining your key thoughts can be more difficult than you expect. There are, more often than not, automatic thoughts that are a part of the way we think about particular events and experiences. We may not even be conscious of some of these.

One way to identify unhelpful thoughts is to pay close attention to emotional changes and use these as a cue for analysing the thinking that accompanies them. If you notice any anxiety or tension before your hospital appointment, for example, ask yourself; 'What am I thinking about right now?' To start with, identify three or four thoughts that worry you most about living with cancer and make a note of them. The next step is to use alternative information to check how realistic the thoughts are. If the thoughts that make you anxious are unhelpful, use the technique which follows to challenge them and replace them with a more helpful way of thinking. You may have other anxious thoughts and it is important that you try and identify each of these.

Listing unhelpful thoughts

- 'I can't cope any more.'
- 'I must appear strong all the time otherwise people will think I am weak.'
- 'I have no energy to work – I feel useless and fed up.'
- 'My illness is causing my family undue worry.'
- 'I am a bad parent, partner, son or daughter.'
- 'I don't feel well – the cancer is getting worse.'
- 'I must not ask the doctors too many questions – they are so busy and I can't be seen to be demanding.'

There are many different ways to think about illness and your way may not be the only way. Worry and sadness may result if you don't sometimes challenge your beliefs and thoughts, particularly those that are negative. The techniques here may help you to break the vicious cycle.

For example, suppose you need to take sick leave from work during your treatment and are anxious about telling your boss. You may be convinced that you will lose your job despite a previous excellent attendance record. Is this really the case? In this and other scenarios, questions such as the following may help to challenge inaccurate thinking:

- Why do I feel anxious about taking sick leave from work? (I feel I may be letting my boss or my colleagues down, my boss may have to find temporary cover for me, my job may be under threat.)
- What facts might I be forgetting or ignoring? (My boss has been supportive in the past, I have a good attendance record, I have been advised to take time off to recover from my treatment and have a letter to this effect.)
- What is *not* true about the process of my taking sick leave from work? (It will affect progress or promotion at work, I may lose my job because of this, I will personally offend my boss or my colleagues.)
- What's the worst thing that can happen? (My work is put on hold for a couple of months, my boss can't find temporary cover for me, I will feel guilty and uncomfortable.)
- What's the best way to handle the anxiety associated with requesting sick leave? (Practise controlled breathing and relaxation techniques to reduce anxiety (see Chapter 6), distract yourself from dwelling on unrealistic outcomes, talk to close friends and family about your situation.)

Challenge anxieties

It may be helpful to list each of your current worries and then go over them, one by one. When you come across a misconception, encourage more realistic thoughts by asking yourself:

- Are my assumptions true or are my anxious feelings leading me to expect the worst?

- Am I falling into the trap of any of the common thinking errors (pp. 26–8)?
- Do I have evidence to support the way I'm thinking? If not, are there alternative thoughts I can have?
- Is there a more helpful or realistic way of thinking?

Try to address each of your anxious thoughts in turn, and even if you find it challenging at first, to generate alternatives to unhelpful thoughts.

Use a format like Table 3.1 to list these.

Once you have identified a worrying thought and constructed an alternative version, the final stage is to put your new way of thinking into practice. It may be difficult to break the habit of

Table 3.1 Anxious thoughts

Anxious thoughts	Alternative thoughts
I don't feel good – the cancer is getting worse.	While it is true that I don't feel very good, this does not necessarily mean that my cancer is getting worse. I could be coming down with something or maybe it is due to tiredness from the cancer treatment. I could speak to a nurse or doctor in the oncology team to get advice on how to manage physical symptoms.
I can't cope any more.	Although I feel stressed and anxious about the situation, I have managed to cope so far. It may help to spend more time on relaxation and positive activities as this may help me feel revitalized and less stressed about my illness.
I have no energy to work – I feel fed up and useless.	Just because I can't work full-time at present does not mean that I am useless. Taking a break could also re-invigorate me. I could also do some work from home or check emails. I could still do some work even though I am not feeling 100 per cent.

anxious thought patterns. You may need to practise alternative thinking for some time before you notice significant changes to the way you feel. Keeping a list of your common negative thoughts and associated alternative ones may help. You can then refer to the list in situations that make you feel upset or anxious – when waiting for test results, for example, or considering telling family and friends about how things are progressing. It is better to direct your energy into actively planning a constructive approach that you know will reduce your anxiety.

> Ian became depressed shortly after receiving a diagnosis of neck cancer. He had lost his step-father to lung cancer five years earlier. Ian was convinced that he too would die from cancer (*interpretation*) despite having been given a positive prognosis by the medical team. He spent the majority of his days sleeping and would rarely answer calls from his friends and family (*behaviour*). Ian felt sad (*emotion*) when thinking that he might not live to see his two nephews grow up (*negative thought*). He was also terrified by the prospect of dying and would often imagine death to be a painful experience (*worry*). He eventually sought help from his GP, who referred him to a psychologist. Working with the psychologist, Ian realized that he had probably developed a fear of cancer after watching his step-father gradually losing his battle with the illness and had come to assume that all forms of cancer are terminal. He began to identify some of the underlying beliefs about cancer and dying which may have triggered his depression. He learned and practised various techniques to help him challenge the assumption that his cancer was not curable. Five years later, Ian is happily married with his first child on the way.

Redirecting your thoughts

Another approach to managing anxious thoughts is to focus your attention on something other than the current worry. Subconsciously we may be attributing our feelings of fear and anxiety about our health to personal failings, and may also direct this to the world around us or to other people. These thoughts all contribute to the way that we formulate our problems. Some are automatic thoughts to which we give particular attention in situations where we experience health anxiety. Learning to control the direction of your attention and refocusing it on other aspects of your experience may improve mood and reduce anxiety.

When you pay too much attention to anxiety-provoking sensations and images, your ability to process information around you is limited. Intentionally directing your attention away from anxious threats does not mean suppressing your thoughts. Instead, you can master what you pay attention to when your anxiety is triggered, so you feel more comfortable.

Try and identify the distractions that are most likely to work for you. Plan to use them next time you find yourself dealing with a difficult situation, such as waiting to see your consultant, but keep in mind that some distractions can inadvertently add pressure. If you plan to use your work to distract you from thinking about your treatment, for example, you may feel more stressed if you fail to concentrate effectively. It is important to choose realistic goals that aren't too ambitious and don't add to your stress.

Some people find it helpful to use simple distraction techniques, such as doing a crossword, talking to a friend, watching TV, reading a magazine or flicking through a photo album.

Music can provide an effective and welcome reprieve from internal anxieties. Play some music that you enjoy and try to focus on what you are hearing rather than on yourself or on what is going on around you. It may be difficult at first to shut it all out, but with practice this type of concentration can be a tool to reduce distress and increase feelings of relaxation and calm when worry threatens to overwhelm us.

Others may prefer to meditate on their environment, focusing on what is around them. It requires concentration to take in all the detail, and this can distract from difficult emotions. Submerging ourselves in what is around us can be surprisingly calming.

See Chapter 6 for more on techniques for relaxation, such as controlled breathing, muscle relaxation and imagery.

Cognitive behavioural therapy, which we've used in this chapter to help challenge distressing thoughts, is not a miraculous 'quick fix' to cure all your emotional problems. Rather, it gradually allows you to build up your confidence and a repertoire of skills for coping with difficult situations. The next chapter will look at what you do to cope with your cancer and how certain behaviours such as avoidance can be counter-productive.

5

Changing unhelpful behaviours

Some responses to illness may arise because of misconceptions or inaccurate beliefs about our physical symptoms. Avoidance is a classic negative coping reaction to a chronic illness. We may avoid seeing other people or particular activities, or even medical appointments. This can perpetuate feelings of anxiety and depression.

It's a natural response to try and avoid frightening or difficult situations. In many situations, though, avoidance can paradoxically increase our feelings of anxiety. We may be avoiding everyday activities that we enjoy or that distract us, avenues for support from our friends and colleagues or help from professionals if we avoid talking about how we feel.

> Sarah, aged 42, had been afraid of needles since early childhood. During her last appointment at her oncology clinic, she experienced intense anxiety when the nurse wanted to take a blood sample. Sarah became nervous and tearful (*emotions*) and remembers thinking to herself 'I can't cope,' 'They will miss my vein,' 'It will be painful,' 'I will faint' (*negative thoughts*). She became tearful and begged the nurse to leave the blood test until another day (*avoidance*). The nurse sat and talked with Sarah about how she was feeling about the blood test and coping with cancer generally. Sarah became more settled and relaxed (*physical symptoms*) and agreed to have the blood test. The nurse suggested that Sarah might discuss her fear of needles with a psychologist. With the help of the psychologist, Sarah was gradually able to challenge the catastrophic thoughts (*change thoughts*) and anxious feelings (*change symptoms*) she experienced during injections and blood samples. She eventually overcame her needle phobia and no longer dreaded her clinic appointments.

While avoidance can be helpful in the short term because it gets us out of having to face up to something, it may not be in our long-term interests. Some people go to great lengths to avoid particular situations and are never really aware of the toll that this takes on them. Think about a time when you delayed taking action until the last minute. You may have been saved some discomfort in the short term, but it is also likely that the task you avoided will have played on your mind. It may have also affected others around you. There are other unhelpful reactions too, some of which can be quite destructive. Some people turn to short-term relief from their worries through alcohol or recreational drug use.

Before you can begin to address these negative ways to cope, it helps to have a clearer understanding of the way you behave in certain situations.

Assess your weekly activities

This activity-monitoring exercise relies on a diary approach. Try writing down all the things you do during the day, even simple activities like making a cup of coffee or returning a phone call. Take stock and try to appreciate the stresses and pressures you are under at this time. You could use a format like Table 5.1, recording what you did in each period of the day, including when you ate and rested.

Table 5.1 Monitoring your activities

	Monday	Tuesday	Wednesday	Thursday	Friday	Saturday	Sunday
Morning 7.00–13.00							
Afternoon 13.00–18.00							
Evening 18.00–23.00							

On reflection, you may see that you are doing less now than you did before you had cancer. This wouldn't be surprising. On the other hand, you may find that you are trying to do just as much or even more than you used to. These changes or even lack of change could be because of particular coping behaviours such as avoidance or denial. Excessive activity may be contributing to your tiredness and frustration and other behaviours may be perpetuating your negative mood or emotions. Have a look at your diary to see if you can see any typical behaviour recurring. Are you:

- throwing yourself into doing things all the time so there are no opportunities to reflect about what you're going through;
- being overly aware and excessively checking for symptoms of cancer worsening or coming back;
- avoiding exercise, socializing or everyday activities because you feel too tired and lack the motivation to do anything;
- pushing people away emotionally and rejecting offers of support;
- seeing more of people, becoming dependent on others or avoiding being on your own for fear of your feelings;
- drinking too much, perhaps to try and block out persistent and painful emotional reactions?

While a reduction in activity may be necessary or inevitable, particularly around treatments or after surgery, continuing to do some tasks and keeping some engagements can be helpful, especially if they are things that you enjoy. Try planning your weekly activities in advance. This will give you a sense of control over your life and help to pre-empt problems. If you find that you are doing too much, try to concentrate on those activities that are less demanding and more enjoyable. It is always helpful to plan carefully around treatment days so that you're not overdoing it when you aren't feeling well. If we have to undergo surgery, notice how we are encouraged to mobilize soon after an operation. This has been found to help us recover physically much sooner and to improve mood and confidence, which also aids overall recovery.

Activities which can contribute towards feelings of health and emotional safety include:

- talking openly with friends and family;
- being proactive about managing your illness and associated challenges (this includes reading about cancer and asking nursing and medical staff about your treatments and how to deal with any side-effects);
- enjoying regular activities such as meeting friends, spending time with your family, going shopping, gardening or going for walks, if possible;
- trying to deal with negative thoughts by identifying them, reflecting on them and challenging them, rather than accepting them;

- sharing or externalizing your experiences through keeping a diary or through a support group where you can learn about how others are coping with their illness.

Gareth, a single man in his late twenties, had recently moved from Liverpool to London to further his career. About four months into the new job, Gareth became troubled by nosebleeds, a sore throat that would not go away and frequent headaches. He was later diagnosed with throat cancer and began his treatment at an oncology clinic shortly after-wards. Although Gareth's family visited him every weekend, he felt lonely during the week as he did not have anyone to talk to now that he had taken sick leave from work. Gareth's mother suggested that he contacted Macmillan Cancer Support to see whether they would be able to offer some form of counselling, but Gareth felt embarrassed at the thought of sharing intimate details about his current situation with a stranger. After a difficult week, however, he finally plucked up courage and called them. He was invited to attend a cancer support group the following evening, so that he could meet other people whose experience might be similar to his own. Gareth was still not convinced and felt nervous about the thought of attending a group, but did attend the support group and was surprised at how comfortable he felt during the meeting. Over the next few months, he attended regularly and became friendly with two other members, meeting up with them outside the group.

Understanding your coping strategies

Once you have a list of your key behaviours, you can then assess what contribution they make to your overall coping. Are they unhelpful or helpful strategies? The negative coping strategies may be more difficult to identify. We've seen that our health-related behaviours are often linked in subtle ways to our underlying beliefs about illness. They are shaped by so many factors, many of which are intangible, such as our personalities, our upbringing and our experiences. Try to reflect on all your coping strategies. Where it makes sense, think of the activities you listed in your weekly diary as a sequence of events, in an 'ABC analysis' like this:

- *An activating event (A)*: this is an event that triggers thoughts or feelings. It can be internal (low self-esteem, worrying about the future) or external (challenging situations, people, objects, an invitation, being kept waiting to see your doctor).

- *Your beliefs (B)*: these are your thoughts in relation to the event. Some of them will be automatic thoughts, while others are related to your attitudes or the meanings you give to circumstances or experiences. You may believe, for example, that cancer or other illness is some form of punishment for leading a stressful life.
- *The consequences (C)*: these are your *behaviours* and *feelings* as a consequence of your beliefs. How did you behave in response to the activating event? Was this a constructive response? Are you able to define any emotions too? How did you feel?

To begin with, try to record events that trigger thoughts and behaviours and the beliefs that are associated with them. Here are some examples to help you get started:

Example 1

1 *A:* You are visiting the hospital for a consultation with your oncologist.

2 *B:* You avoid telling him or her about persistent feelings of pain because you believe that to show you are in pain may suggest you are 'weak' or a 'troublesome patient'.

3 *C:* Your pain persists and you feel annoyed at yourself for not asking for guidance on how to manage this.

Example 2

1 *A:* You have an argument with your partner.

2 *B:* You believe you are right and don't feel that it is necessary to compromise on your position.

3 *C:* As a consequence, there is a tense atmosphere in the house all day and you avoid each other. The whole day is written off; you ruminate about your relationship and you feel sad.

There may be a series of responses to a situation that you feel are negative, and wish to change. Instead of trying to tackle all these at once, break them down and move from more general problem areas to a clear target problem that you can work on. If, for example, you think you are not coping well at work, you could ask yourself what precisely you are finding difficult (e.g. Is concentration a problem because you are worried or distressed? Do you have difficulty completing tasks while taking time off for clinic appointments?). The answers to these questions will provide you with a specific problem to target. In the case of work difficulties, a solution might be to reduce your hours of work or take some time off until you feel better. You can use this process to make any problem area clearer. If, for example, you feel that you are 'pushing people away emotionally', you can be more precise about this issue by asking yourself in what ways you are pushing other people away. You may be avoiding friends or family, declining offers of support, being dismissive and irritable towards others or even being overly independent. Your response to this question gives you a precise behaviour to work on. The point is to work through the vagaries of your negative thoughts and identify precise behaviours that can be addressed. When you have done this, you can identify targets to work towards.

> Richard, aged 28, enjoyed drinking alcohol with his friends at his local pub at weekends. When he was diagnosed with prostate cancer, the visits to the pub became more frequent and Richard would often drink large amounts of alcohol on his own. One day when he was attending the clinic for treatment, Richard fell asleep in the waiting area, having consumed three bottles of wine the night before. His breath smelt of alcohol and he looked awful. Richard realized that he needed to cut down on the drinking (*target goal*) because it was interfering with both his physical wellbeing and his quality of life. On reflection, Richard came to appreciate that he had used alcohol (*behaviour*) to quell the frightening prospect of not being able to recover from his cancer (*activating event*). Although Richard had initially thought that drinking helped him to 'block out' health concerns, the excessive use of alcohol had worsened his anxiety and put him at risk of alcohol dependency (*consequence*). Richard was able to stop drinking during the week and would instead watch a movie, visit friends or read a book in the evenings (*alternative behaviours*). He occasionally has a couple of beers when visiting the pub with his friends but he no longer relies on alcohol to cope with the cancer treatment.

The physical impact of the hangovers helped Richard to acknowledge the way his drinking had become problematic. At other times,

Table 5.2 Assessing your solutions

Solution	Advantages	Disadvantages
Go for walks in the park two or three times a week	• It is inexpensive • My level of fitness will increase • I may feel more positive	• Motivation is sometimes difficult • During cancer treatment I may feel physically unwell
Cook a meal for my partner	• My partner will be pleased • I may enjoy cooking; it will give me a sense of achievement • I can use the new cookery book that my friend gave me for my birthday	• Shopping may tire me

it may not be so easy to identify the types of behaviours that are unhelpful, especially if the consequences are less marked and therefore more difficult to notice.

Once you have a realistic target for change, think about things you can do to reach it. Brainstorming may help you to come up with as many ideas as possible. Although some may seem simplistic or trivial, this doesn't matter. The key is to record all the solutions that you can think of. Ask a friend, family member or a counsellor to help if you get stuck. The following questions can help you to think about practical and realistic solutions:

• What are the alternatives to your current behaviour?
• What advice would you give a friend who was facing similar challenges?
• Have you encountered a similar problem in the past, and if so, what did you do to overcome it?
• Is there anything else that you could be doing to help you change the behaviour?

Weigh up the advantages and disadvantages of the solutions you have come up with. This will help you to choose the most realistic one. Table 5.2 gives some examples of the advantages and disadvantages of specific behavioural solutions. Use a similar table to fill in your own.

Incorporating positive changes

Once you have a solution that you feel will work for you, the next step is to integrate the new behaviour into your daily schedule. You can use the ABC analysis (see p. 42) to help you monitor the effects. Don't give up or feel you have failed if you are struggling to change particular coping strategies. They are not always easy and may need practice. Also, your health circumstances may change and you may need to be flexible. Look for new ways to facilitate change, perhaps by setting smaller or more realistic goals for yourself. Expect some setbacks as these are a normal part of change. It is only natural to feel anxious as you are learning new ways to cope and to let go of habitual behaviours.

Tom's experience shows how overloading yourself can have a negative effect.

> Tom is 42 and has recently been diagnosed with a brain cancer called a glioma. As the managing director of a large financial corporation, he continued to spend long hours at work and would socialize afterwards, even shortly after undergoing surgery to remove the tumour. The radiotherapy he had as part of his treatment made him feel increasingly tired and he would often experience nausea and headaches. He didn't allow himself to address these, feeling that they should not stop him from 'keeping busy'. He would often be the last person to leave work despite feeling physically exhausted. Some weeks later, Tom experienced intense heart palpitations and breathing difficulties at work. He initially thought he was having a heart attack but was later told by his GP that he had suffered from a panic attack. The GP referred Tom to a counsellor who helped him to understand the nature of his panic attacks and to accept both his illness and the limits that the treatment was putting on him. His counsellor encouraged him to 'listen to his body' and get the rest he needed to reduce the current stress levels that were the cause of his panic attack.

Tom's experience helps reinforce the need for a healthy balance in our activities when we are unwell. He wanted to continue working during his treatment and was able to do so. Initially, this helped him to retain a sense of control over his life and continue doing the things that motivated him and gave him his sense of purpose. The combination of his heavy workload, the effects of a difficult treatment and the expected emotional impact of having cancer proved too much for him to cope with, however.

This chapter aimed to help you see how your behaviours are part of your coping style and how certain negative ones, such as avoidance, can be counter-productive. It is important to reflect upon what you do and try to gain a better understanding of how you respond to thoughts about having cancer. This will help you to identify unhelpful behaviours and can allow you to adapt them, or replace them with more constructive ones. The next chapter focuses on the physical symptoms of stress and anxiety.

6

Learning to relax

In this chapter we first focus on controlled breathing exercises before moving on to releasing physical tension and relaxing the body and mind. All are important skills that can help you feel calmer and more comfortable when you are faced with stress, anxiety, unpleasant physical symptoms and uncertainty.

Stress and anxiety are normal responses to worrying situations. Often, people who are feeling particularly anxious or stressed may misinterpret some of their physical symptoms as being potentially harmful or life-threatening – 'catastrophizing'. This can lead to

Table 6.1 Misinterpretations of physical symptoms

Physical symptom	What is happening	Misinterpretations
Shallow rapid breathing, lightheadedness, dizziness	Hyperventilation: you are over-breathing. The level of carbon dioxide in your blood is lower than it should be and this is causing the symptoms you are experiencing.	I can't breathe, I am suffocating.
Muscle pain	Tension: muscular tension which can be a result of stress, can lead to headaches and pains.	The treatment is unbearable, the cancer is getting worse.
Nausea	Many things can cause nausea including anxiety, hyperventilation, low blood sugar, etc.	I will collapse in front of my doctor. I will faint. I will look foolish in front of others.
Sweating, trembling, hot and flushed	Many things can cause these symptoms, including hypoglycaemia, overheating, the menopause, the effects of some drugs.	I can't cope with my illness. I feel more frightened and depressed.

heightened anxiety which may increase the severity of symptoms. The resulting symptoms reinforce the belief that there is something to worry about, and so a vicious circle develops. *Catastrophizing and anticipating negative outcomes have been linked to more severe pain and increased fatigue in some cancer patients. However, again it's important to point out that feelings don't 'cause' cancer.*

Unpleasant physical symptoms can be frightening and distressing and can give rise to two challenges: the effects of anxiety, coupled with a fear of experiencing these symptoms. These have the further effect of reinforcing one another. Anticipation of physical discomfort, nausea, pain, sweating, breathing difficulties or tightening in the chest area, to name a few, can produce the stress that reinforces these bodily sensations. Table 6.1 is an example of the many exaggerated interpretations of physical discomfort.

While being relaxed may help us to tackle the anxiety that underpins some of these physical responses or that occurs as the reaction to them, it isn't necessarily easy to achieve. Often it will need to be learned or re-learned if stressful circumstances have made us forget how to relax. This happened to Janet, when her physical symptoms of anxiety interfered with her ability to deal with her cancer.

Janet had always been prone to worry and described herself as quite an anxious person. When she was diagnosed with cancer, the anxiety got progressively worse. Despite not having suffered too many physical symptoms in the past, Janet became troubled by frequent hyperventilation, excessive sweating and intense muscular tension. She finally sought help from a psychologist after suffering a panic attack on her way to pick up her eight-year-old daughter from school. As she and the psychologist explored her cancer experience, Janet began to identify some of the factors which might have contributed to her physical discomfort. In particular, she understood that the stress of dealing with her cancer and worrying about her daughter might have caused her previous anxieties to re-emerge, and might even have reinforced them. Janet learned and practised deep breathing and relaxation techniques to help reduce the physical symptoms of anxiety. The psychologist also helped Janet to identify and challenge anxiety-provoking thoughts. She met the psychologist on three occasions and continued to practise various relaxation sequences on a daily basis. It was not long until Janet noticed that her breathing was becoming much better and that the excessive sweating had ceased. She no longer felt terrorized by the intense muscular tension she used to endure and was therefore able to enjoy social activities with her daughter again.

A range of techniques can help you minimize feelings of anxiety and stress, and you will need to find an approach that suits you.

You may find it helpful to assess your own levels of stress and anxiety before you move on to the relaxation exercises. Table 6.2 may be a useful monitor of the effectiveness of the breathing and muscle-relaxing exercises which follow.

Table 6.2 Monitoring the effects of relaxation

How tense, stressed, and/or anxious do I feel? How intense is my pain?	Before relaxation 1 (low) – 10 (high)	After relaxation 1 (low) – 10 (high)
Tense		
Stressed		
Anxious		
Pain		

Controlling your breathing

We tend to over-breathe when we are tense. This mild form of hyperventilation is perfectly normal and is our body's way of ensuring that our muscles are primed in case they need to react quickly. However, continued rapid breathing can lead to physical symptoms that may be unpleasant and even frightening if a full-blown panic attack ensues. Try to imagine the following scenario:

You are sitting in the waiting room at the hospital about to be called in for your first chemotherapy treatment. You are feeling anxious about this, and in response your heart beats faster and you begin to breathe more rapidly. You soon feel hot and sweaty. Your throat feels dry and you start to feel nauseated and jittery. You are aware that you now look anxious and you wonder what is happening to you and whether you might lose control.

There are two main things going on here. Your initial anxiety about your treatment has triggered a nervous response that is normal, but you develop a secondary anxiety about the symptoms you are experiencing. You can pre-empt hyperventilation and associated symptoms of increased stress and anxiety by learning to manage your breathing in situations that may provoke them. This can be done anywhere: on your way to a clinic appointment, before or after treatment and when you are on your own and feeling upset. If you can, practise twice a day for about ten minutes each time in a quiet place free from distractions and noise. You may feel more relaxed if you do this on your own. You can then learn to apply this new skill to situations where you experience greater emotional distress.

- Sit down, with your hands relaxed on either side of your body, or lie flat on your back. Find a position where you feel physically comfortable.
- It may help to loosen tight clothing and remove your shoes.
- Let your shoulder blades drop, press your back into the chair or ground and close your eyes.
- Start by taking a deep inward breath through your nose, then slowly exhale out of your mouth. Continue to breathe in through your nose and out of your mouth five or six more times.
- Try counting slowly from 1 to 4 when you inhale. Do the same when you exhale, so that you are breathing evenly in a slow and focused way.
- Focus on the sensations of the air entering your nose.
- Put your right hand on your abdomen and let it rest there lightly. As you breathe in, feel the way your chest and abdomen rise. Breathe out fully, noting the way they fall.
- Your heart-beat should be slowing down and your arms and legs should feel more relaxed. Continue to count slowly from 1 to 4 on each inhalation and exhalation.
- You may find it helpful to visualize the tension leaving your body as you breathe out. Imagine that you are pushing all of your tension out through your lungs. Let it flow out through your mouth and away from you, and focus on the quiet and peace around you.
- Slowly open your eyes. Continue to breathe gently and evenly in through your nose and out through your mouth. Raise your arms and stretch your body upwards if you are in a seated position. If you are lying down, flex your arms and legs downwards and gently move back up into a seated position.

Controlled breathing and relaxation can be surprisingly difficult at first, but after practising several times you should be able to switch to correct breathing whenever you feel anxious. Practise the breathing exercise when you can, particularly in distracting situations.

Muscle relaxation

Stress can manifest in many ways, but many of us will hold a lot of our tension in our muscles. We are not always conscious of the physical tension we carry around. Leah, for example, had noticed a gradual build-up of stress, tiredness and muscular pain after she started her treatment for cervical cancer.

> There were days when Leah struggled to get out of bed in the morning because she felt so exhausted. The doctors had warned her that the treatment could lead her to tire easily and that she might experience some physical discomfort. She knew that she should try and get as much rest as possible, but this was not always possible. There were so many things to organize with the house and the children. The worry of not caring adequately for her family would often play on her mind when she lay in bed during the day. Her muscles, especially in the neck area, were tense and painful, while her feet looked swollen. She visited a physiotherapist, who gave her some light physical exercises that she could practise on a daily basis. Although this took away the stiffness in her limbs, Leah often found that the pain and the tiredness got worse when she was feeling worried and stressed about her health and family. Her husband was always telling her that the children were fine. He had also suggested that they hire someone to help with daily household chores but Leah refused. She wanted to do it herself, just as she always had in the past. This allowed her to retain a sense of 'normality' along-side the uncertainty of living with cervical cancer.

The following exercise can help to increase your awareness of bodily tension, which can then be a cue to trying relaxation techniques. The sequence is quite simple and encourages you to focus on all parts of your body. At first, it may be best to try the relaxation exercise while you are lying down, though sitting in a chair works just as well. Once you are confident using the technique, you can use it in any situations you find stressful. The controlled breathing we talked about on p. 50 may enhance your sense of relaxation and calmness.

The basic steps:

1 Tense your muscles as hard as you can and concentrate on feeling the strain of them.
2 After you have held the tension for five seconds, release it and relax your muscles for 15 seconds. Make a mental note of the differences between the tense and relaxed state of your muscles.

Use this basic technique on each of the muscle groups we list below. Remember to breathe gently and evenly throughout the exercise, and stop if you are in excessive pain.

Hands Clench your left hand and make a tight fist. Then relax your left hand – let it sink towards the ground. Do the same with your right hand.

Arms Tense your whole arm. Imagine that you are holding a set of weights in your hand. Bring the lower half of your arm upwards as this will make it easier to flex your arm. Relax for 15 seconds. Repeat with your other arm.

Face Frown to tense your forehead and eyebrows. Clench your jaw. Relax for 15 seconds and repeat.

Neck and shoulders Drop your chin down towards your chest. Raise your shoulders up towards your neck as hard as you can. Hold for 15 seconds and then relax. Repeat the process one more time. As your shoulders release, feel your shoulder blades drop.

Abdomen Clench your stomach muscles. Hold this for five seconds and then relax for 15 seconds. Repeat the tensing and relax again.

Thighs Relax your upper body. Tighten your thigh muscles by squeezing your buttocks and thighs together. Relax for 15 seconds before you repeat the process again.

Legs Bend your feet downwards so that your toes are pointing towards the floor. There should be a tightening sensation in the back of your leg muscles. Relax for 15 seconds. Then bend your feet the other way so that your toes are pointing upwards. You should feel a light tension in the front part of your legs. Relax.

Your whole body Tense all the above body parts at once. You should feel a tension in your hands, face area, neck and shoulders, abdomen, thighs and legs. Relax for 15 seconds and then repeat this process once more.

Take care not to over-tense your muscles as this may cause you more discomfort or even injury. Before you stand up, gently stretch and move your arms and legs to get your circulation going properly again. Avoid sudden or jerky movements and, when you are ready, take your time standing up. With practice you should be able to use this relaxation technique in any situation. At first it may be difficult to ignore the distractions around you, but learning to relax in a range of different environments can be helpful.

Deep relaxation

This is a visualization exercise, so you will need to have in your mind a soothing, relaxing scenario. Here are some suggestions that will help get you started: You could recall:

- a place you have visited with which you associate peace and calm: a deserted beach; a holiday home; a garden; a view; watching and listening to the rain drum against your window; the scenery during a visit to the countryside;
- a poem; the lyrics of a favourite song; a word or phrase that brings positive images to your mind;
- an object, person, movie or picture that you particularly like.

Follow these steps:

- Sit comfortably with your eyes closed.
- Focus on your breathing; listen to the sounds of your breath.
- When you inhale, fill your lungs completely with air before exhaling slowly. You are aiming to deepen and slow your breathing.
- As you breathe, focus on your mental picture and try to visualize what you can see, hear and smell. Allow your mind and body to relax and try to let go of all of your tension.
- Be aware of the way your body feels as you relax. Continue the exercise for 15 to 20 minutes.

- When you have finished, open your eyes and stay sitting for a minute or two.
- Slowly move your limbs to get your circulation going.

Many people find that deep breathing, progressive muscle relaxation and visualizations help them to relax. There are other techniques, too. Regular exercise has a number of benefits, including relaxation. It increases blood circulation to the muscles and leads to release of endorphins (the 'happy hormones') from the brain. If you have cancer and want to start exercising or to continue with physical activities you have previously enjoyed, talk to your doctors about this to ensure that it is safe to do so. The next chapter focuses on the impact of living with cancer on the wider family.

7

Enhancing family relationships

The psychological effects of cancer can be as challenging and sometimes as devastating to family members as they are for the person who carries the burden of illness. When it comes to coping with cancer, the state of our family relationships as well as how our partner adjusts to the situation may matter more to us than anything else. Where close relationships come to feel tense, strained, emotionally distant or volatile, these changes can tip the balance and make us susceptible to anxiety, depression, hopelessness, and even worse. The way in which cancer psychologically impacts upon those around us, as well as how they in turn support us, is complex. An understanding of how relationships can be affected paves the way for more open communication and improved support, both of which have been linked to more favourable health outcomes.

Family reactions to cancer

We first need to clarify what is meant by the term 'family'. These days, it has come to include a broad range of relationships and takes into account the diverse social networks and cultural backgrounds reflected in modern society. 'Family' has come to include not only blood relations, but others such as those who share a household, or who are by the individual's definition his or her closest relatives or those who provide the greatest social and emotional support. This includes common-law partners, civil partners in same-sex relationships, close friends, in-laws and others that people may wish to include as members of their 'family'. Those whom we relate to by choice may be as much family as those who are related by birth. We know that whomever we choose to call 'family', these key figures in our lives may be just as affected by the same emotional and practical issues that affect anyone who has cancer.

Why should we include a section in this book on family support? One reason is that no illness occurs completely in isolation, and how the individual reacts to and copes with a cancer diagnosis may, in turn, affect how family members cope. Furthermore, gaining some insight into how family members react can be important in understanding the impact of the illness on the individual. How one copes influences how the other copes. This process is circular and new patterns of caregiving can emerge where there is serious illness in a family member.

It can also lead to greater distancing between some family members who withdraw socially and emotionally. This can be very difficult to cope with just when you were hoping for greater closeness and support. Withdrawing can be due to:

1 feeling fearful of what has happened and what may lie ahead;
2 not wanting to be burdened with providing support;
3 an irrational fear of 'catching' the same illness;
4 a fear of being 'infected' emotionally by the distress and painful feelings that may accompany ill health within the family (this can also be as a result of a selfish need not to be 'held back' in one's life by having to be a caregiver within the family);
5 where it exists, the effects of social stigma by being associated with someone who has cancer;
6 where some members simply do not want to get too close to their relatives because of painful experiences from past patterns in family relationships.

All these issues can cause extra hardship for the person trying to cope with a cancer diagnosis.

There are three different main kinds of support that family members can offer and provide. These include:

1 practical support – such as help with mobility, doing the cooking and washing, assisting with visits to the doctor or clinic, and help with changing a dressing;
2 financial support – help with income and living expenses, going to work to make up loss of income due to the family member's inability to work, paying prescription charges and for private health care;

3 social and emotional support – being there and available to talk and listen, accompanying the person to a chemotherapy session, giving support and offering encouragement and at times offering a shoulder to cry on.

It may be neither possible nor appropriate for every family member to provide all three kinds of support. Instead, different family members might be better placed to offer some aspects of support, or it may be necessary to access support from outside the immediate family. Reduced access to social, emotional and financial support may be the result of previous schisms, tensions, patterns and difficulties in family relationships. It may be difficult to ask for help from family members who have withdrawn or turned their backs on one another. This can raise tensions within the family, as some members are excluded from caregiving while others find that that they have to take on twice the burden to fill the gaps.

How to organize family support

- Think what you need from people. Draw up a list: healthcare issues, practical support, financial concerns, emotional issues and, if relevant, support for children.
- Ask people directly! Waiting for them to offer could prove frustrating and disappointing. Sometimes people are unsure as to whether they will upset you by offering to help.
- Try to spread the demands around so as not to overburden any one person. If necessary, draw up a rota.
- Discuss your concerns with those who offer to help but who don't follow up. Don't let your disappointments fester.
- Remember to thank people. This reinforces their helping behaviour.
- Try to keep up as many self-care activities as you can: they help to maintain esteem and confidence.
- Ask doctors and nurses what may lie ahead, so you can try to plan ahead for problems or crises.

Of course, the advent of a serious illness such as cancer need not drive away family members. It can sometimes start to heal rifts in family relationships. People can experience new patterns of care and emotional closeness. While illness is never welcome, its effects can change how family members relate to one another and bring out hidden strengths and warmth not previously seen.

Telling the family

Support cannot be given, however, where illness has not been disclosed. Telling the family is difficult and can be upsetting for all concerned. How we disclose news of a cancer diagnosis and to whom within the family sheds light on three important dynamics within relationships. These are:

- who is defined as close family;
- who is being 'protected' and shielded from the news which could unduly upset them, such as children or elderly relatives; and
- who is excluded from knowing about the condition, which may reflect hostile or conflicted relationships.

Telling others within the family is usually a big challenge for the individual for several reasons. This is because it signals the potential for changes in the family's structure, roles and relationships, patterns of care and support, and it raises the possibility (and sometimes too the inevitability) of actual loss, as well as indirect changes in other family members. These include the possibility of having to cancel or postpone one's own plans and future aspirations.

Disclosure of illness – the act of telling others the nature of the medical problem and what it means – is not always a carefully planned event. Sometimes it comes to light because a child has seen a letter from the clinic or a partner overhears a telephone discussion with a doctor. At these times, you may be confronted with questions which need to be answered either in a completely honest way or with the minimum of information, in order to begin to build up knowledge and understanding over time. Disclosure is usually *selective*. This means that we do not normally tell everyone everything at once. Most people tell only selected family and friends at first and may only give limited information. Maybe nothing more is available at the time, or perhaps you are 'testing' others to see how they react before sharing more difficult or emotionally painful aspects. For this reason, disclosure is also usually *incremental*. It is part of an ongoing process. We may update what we tell according to what we know and what we want others to know about our health.

It is extremely common within families to observe a complex coping 'dance' between the person with cancer and his or her close friends and family. It is a subtle, two-way and circular process. The person with cancer may take cues from how others are coping and adjusting, which in turn affects how he or she copes. For example, other family members may cope better if they see that their relative is coping well, which in turn raises their sprits and helps the person to feel better. Understandably, some family members may find it difficult to maintain a supportive outlook in the face of illness, and this in turn affects how the individual copes.

While in some families disclosure of illness increases closeness between family members, the changes that follow are sometimes stressful and some family members have difficulty adjusting to the roles that they have to adopt. In some relationships, the advent of illness means that the pattern changes to more of a caring role. Alan's story illustrates the impact disclosure had on his family relationships.

Alan is a gay man who first tested HIV positive 14 years ago. He developed lymphoma – a type of cancer commonly associated with advanced HIV disease – six months ago. He has been in a relationship for 16 years and reports that his partner has been very supportive since the diagnosis. Alan has always been open about his sexuality and had been 'out' to his family for many years. He suspected that he was HIV positive as he had an 'open' relationship with his partner and had had other sexual partners, taking significant risks by not having protected intercourse. Since the couple always used condoms when having sex together, Alan had not infected his partner.

In spite of his suspicions, Alan found it difficult to come to terms with the diagnosis and feared that his partner, close friends and family would reject him. He was also concerned that his family would be angry with him: they were very fond of his partner and might not understand their 'open' relationship. Alan initially told his partner the diagnosis, as well as two close friends. They, in turn, encouraged him to tell his mother and his older brother and sister (his father had died).

There was wide variation in the responses to disclosure and these also changed over time. One friend was particularly concerned about how long Alan would survive and felt at a loss as to how to be supportive. Over a period of several months, he began to withdraw from the friendship and would only make telephone calls to Alan rather than visit him. They eventually lost all contact. Another friend appeared to become overly caring and intrusive, but Alan found that by discussing what was helpful with his well-meaning friend he was able to 'breathe' again in the relationship.

His mother felt unsure of the amount and nature of support to offer Alan. Although they had a reasonably good relationship, they had no track record for dealing with sensitive and emotional issues between them, apart from his father's death. Discovering what worked for mother and son in this difficult time was new territory for both. His mother tried to put on a brave face, but below the surface she was at a loss, wondering how she would cope in her later years without Alan's support. His older brother blamed the illness on her liberal attitude

---

Box 1 How to disclose your cancer diagnosis within the family

- Stop and think before disclosing. Consider how people will react and understand that this will depend on what and how you tell them.
- Choose whom you want, or need, to tell.
- Plan when and where you will tell people (avoid noisy public places, times when there are children around, times when there is little scope for further discussion).
- If there is anything you want from the person, ask directly.
- Emotional expression is normal. People should expect you to be 'real' and display normal emotions and feelings. Encourage these in other people.
- First tell the facts and what you know. Follow this with what is still being investigated and what is unknown, and then tell the person how you feel.
- Consider disclosure as part of a longer-term process: you don't have to say everything at once. You may need to tell more at another time.

towards Alan's homosexuality. Concerned that the stress would affect his own wife's pregnancy, he withdrew from family activities, leaving his mother to be supported by Alan's partner and Alan's sister.

Alan's mother felt that his illness could 'tear apart' the family emotionally and so she tried to appear cheerful in order to help him cope with the diagnosis. This made Alan feel loved and supported, which in turn helped him to stay at work and keep his relationship with his partner. In the coming year, however, she developed Irritable Bowel Syndrome and was referred by her gastro-enterologist to a therapist. The therapist discussed with her the possibility that subjugating her feelings was at a cost to her physical health, and suggested that Alan be invited to join them in a session to discuss their feelings towards each other and the situation.

Box 1 lists some ideas that can help you in planning what to tell family.

Advancing or deteriorating illness can place new stresses on relationships. This may make it more difficult for people to cope and relationships can become strained or emotionally intense.

Susan, the ex-wife of Ben, who was diagnosed with chronic myeloid leukaemia two years ago, told her counsellor that his advancing illness caused her the biggest emotional distress because of the effect it had on him. In spite of the fact that they were divorced, she continued to visit him weekly with their grown-up children:

'The only thing that would make it harder for me to cope with Ben is if he started to deteriorate because I didn't know Ben as a person to give up, to be ill, or to have any problems, and then to see a grown man deteriorate or to see a grown man cry, or, you know, die for something that there should be a cure for, that would be my biggest problem.'

Patterns of care can change in families. Children may become caregivers while grandparents may be called on to support their grown-up child at a time when they would normally be looking forward to retirement.

Dealing with strong or intense emotions in the family

Communication between family members can become strained where serious illness has intruded. Below is a list of suggestions for dealing with strong emotions.

- Accept that intense feelings are normal in the face of illness, even though they may not have been expressed or shown in the family before.
- Allow time for discussion about family members' feelings as well as your own.
- Find helpful ways to deal with intense feelings (go for a walk with that person; hug them; get close; be with them; don't run away). Talk about what can be done or changed to improve things.
- Give people time to adjust and cope.
- Seek counselling from an experienced counsellor or psychologist for yourself as well as for the whole family together to facilitate the safe expression of feelings and to resolve conflict.

Challenges within the family

All families confront a number of challenges where an individual has been diagnosed with a serious health problem, such as cancer. These can be summarized as follows:

- family concern about social stigma and rejection;
- fear of 'infection' (an irrational fear that cancer can be passed on as though it were an infectious condition such as hepatitis or tuberculosis);
- anxiety about talking about the condition with others and people's reactions;
- fear of the impact of disclosure of cancer to others, and also disclosure without the permission of the person;
- guilt and blame arising from past behaviours or lifestyle which might have added to the problem, such as excessive use of alcohol, smoking, anabolic steroids, etc.;
- secrecy between family members about the condition;
- over-protectiveness between family members and also emotional disengagement in others;
- a worsening of existing difficulties in family relationships (such as sibling rivalry or a deteriorating marriage relationship);
- a fear of loss, dying and bereavement – despair about the future;
- a sense of loss about things that can no longer be done within the family;

- denial of problems and of illness as a way of coping, causing tensions and difficulties between family members;
- a fear of loss of sexual functioning between partners.

Challenges to the structure of the family

- There may be loss of productivity, financial hardship and pressure on the breadwinner or demands on someone else in the family to become the breadwinner.
- Patterns of care and support may change: grandparents may have to become carers at a time that they would expect to be cared for; a spouse becomes more of a carer and less of a partner; children may have to take on caregiving responsibilities.
- Sometimes there are difficult decisions to make about whether to have any (or more) children.
- Where the illness can have a fatal outcome, there is the possibility of widowhood, orphanhood or the spectre of a child dying before its parents.

Challenges affecting both the family and others outside

- Frustration with the medical system, professional caregivers and bureaucracy surrounding medical care and financial support for those living with cancer.
- Feeling let down by doctors, nurses, therapists and others who do not seem to listen or who appear to treat all their patients as experiencing the same problem.
- Fear of discrimination at school, work and in social situations.
- Problems keeping up to date with medical advances; the media talking up 'promising treatments' and 'cures' that may not be available or are still experimental.
- Rationed treatments and access to the latest therapies.
- News reports that are distorted or do not reflect your experience.
- Being labelled a 'sufferer' or 'victim' of the condition.

Some of these challenges can continue to affect surviving family members even in the event of a person dying, and afterwards.

For most people, family is the most important source of support in illness. The ideas shared within this chapter may help you to better understand what changes families undergo when a member has cancer and how you can adapt.

8

In sickness and in health – the impact of cancer on couple relationships

One of the most important marriage vows is 'in sickness and in health'. Unless the illness already existed or was foreseen, hardly any of us can be psychologically prepared for the effects of cancer on couple relationships. Some couples find greater closeness and enjoy new levels of intimacy and affection. In contrast, some relationships come to an end because the demands on the couple cannot be met.

The challenge for any couple is to maintain as 'normal' a relationship as possible while coping with cancer. They need to plan ahead, communicate, maintain physical and emotional intimacy and go through normal lifecycle goals (bring up children, prepare for retirement, etc.) in the face of possible deterioration and even loss. These unwelcome changes within relationships may be overlooked by some healthcare professionals, and it is important not to rely on them for counselling or psychological support.

New tensions in relationships

Illness can highlight gender patterns in relationships where, for example, the 'traditional' male provider may become dependent on his female partner, particularly if he is restricted in his ability to work. Also, each partner may have different beliefs, hopes, fears and experiences about illness, coping and how these may affect the relationship. These may not always be shared and may give rise to tensions or disagreements. Valerie, aged 35, had skin cancer:

> I was first diagnosed with skin cancer when I was 38 years old. My skin became itchy and inflamed and one mole in particular caused concern for me and my doctors. It was only quite late after it had spread beyond

66

the original mole that I sought treatment. I remember feeling self-conscious after treatment which involved cutting out quite a bit of my skin around the area.

Having skin cancer came as a real shock. My husband was supportive and even though I felt differently about myself, he tried his best to convince me that I was still beautiful. I, of course, saw nothing but the scar covering my shoulder. There were times when I locked myself inside the house – I was too ashamed and felt that people could see what had happened to my skin.

It affected my marriage the most – I could not stand being physically close to my husband. The thought of getting undressed in front of him was terrifying. I was repulsed by my own appearance. I eventually started sleeping in the guest bedroom – I honestly thought this would save my husband from pretending that he wasn't turning up his nose at my scar. We went a whole year without sexual intimacy. He felt so rejected that he eventually threatened to leave me if I did not talk to someone about my self-loathing. My psychologist was very understanding and helped me deal with my low confidence.

I still find it hard to accept that I had skin cancer but I am gradually finding a way to cope. My husband and I are sharing a bedroom again and I no longer feel the necessity to hide my physical self from him. I still have bad days but these are fewer and less intense than before.

The 'sick role' can feel limiting and indeed intensely constraining for both the individual and the partner. The person who is ill may feel saddened and frustrated by any dependency on a partner. Some people even come to worry that they are unlovable. They may harbour fears that they may be abandoned by their partner, bearing their illness on their own. One consequence of this fear is that they may try to please their partner, avoid discord or fights, or hide some the effects of their illness. Such need for control can give rise to difficult emotions such as bitterness and resentment for having to suppress some of one's true feelings.

A couple may have difficulty 'reading' what is happening in their relationship. Small, niggling issues can be blown out of proportion, leading to increased tension, rows and fights. This may be because they are unsettled by the changes going on in the relationship but have not openly discussed these or planned ways to deal with upsets. Likewise, a couple may avoid any discord in their relationship, 'inflicting' cheeriness on one another and doing everything to keep the peace, despite the fact that this is probably unnatural in even the healthiest relationships!

Couple relationships also undergo change: enjoying extensive care and support from one's partner may be both a relief and welcomed while coming to terms with the cancer diagnosis. However, later on in the relationship, resentment may grow towards the partner who appears to be 'controlling' or 'smothering with kindness'. A couple typically look to one another as well as within themselves to try to 'read' what is happening in their relationship. However, without open communication between the partners about how they are coping, there is the risk that they could misread what the other thinks and feels. This, in turn, can further unbalance the relationship.

Illness can also be an opportunity for more welcome and positive changes and emotional growth. Not every aspect of having a serious illness such as cancer needs to be unpleasant or negative. Both emotional and physical intimacy can increase. Couples can enjoy better communication and mutual support. Some of the small, apparently irrelevant or even unpleasant aspects of daily life can be ignored while the couple focus on themselves and their most important needs. They may do things that they had previously delayed or put off doing.

There may also be a risk of deterioration in the relationship if the illness comes to dominate all aspects of it. Where new roles and patterns surface in relationships and are not openly discussed, the emotional pain can be intense and sometimes overwhelming. It puts each partner, as well as the couple relationship, at greater risk of psychological problems. This includes depression and anxiety as well as all the signs of difficulties in a relationship, such as having frequent rows; less or no sexual intimacy; anger towards one's partner; children misbehaving as a way of deflecting the tensions away from their parents' problems; and having affairs. Some couples say that an illness such as cancer is like having a third (uninvited) person in the relationship. It can also bring to light past lifestyle risks that may have long changed in that person's life, as Peter and Susie's situation illustrates:

Peter, 56, used to smoke, although he gave up some 20 years ago when he married Susie. He also worked abroad as a gold-mine shift supervisor in his early thirties. Peter finally went to see his GP 18 months ago after feeling unwell for some time: he had developed a cough, was tired and had lost weight. He kept putting off making an appointment, and it wasn't until he could no longer work that he finally made an appointment. After a series of tests and scans, he was told that he was suffering from lung cancer. This came as a huge shock as he thought that he had all but eliminated his risk by giving up smoking all those years ago. The doctor explained that he had a higher risk because of his past smoking habit and having worked down a mine, but that it was not possible to tell which had 'caused' his illness. Not only did he have to come to terms with unwelcome news about his health but his and Susie's attention was drawn to aspects of his lifestyle prior to getting married.

Initially Susie was shocked and angry that Peter had 'brought' this problem into their lives. She found it hard to believe or accept that the person she thought she knew so well had not taken better care of himself and also that he had delayed seeking medical attention. A psychologist helped the couple to see that Susie's anger was more a reflection of her not feeling in control of the situation, being fearful of what lay ahead for the family and also possibly being more angry with the cancer than with Peter personally. Susie was able to become more supportive of Peter while he underwent treatment and also to talk openly about her concerns and fears. This improved the couple's relationship and also reduced tension and stress surrounding his illness within the family.

In the face of a threat to a relationship, a couple may start to pull away from one another. Emotions may intensify and become more difficult to bear. Some feelings are particularly complicated. These include a fear of loss, intense anger or jealousy of the other (who appears to have good health), as well as apparently shameful thoughts such as 'I wish he or she would die' as a way of redressing the perceived unfairness and imbalance in the relationship. While the risk of psychological problems may increase in relationships where a partner has cancer, they are not inevitable. If the situation is appropriately managed, greater intimacy can follow.

How can a couple cope and adapt to the challenges of living with cancer?

- See it as 'our' problem, not 'yours'.
- Be willing to address issues and challenges through open communication.
- Revisit the issues and problems in the relationship as things change.
- Talk openly about role changes, emotional intimacy and fear or threat of loss.
- Discuss the impact on sex and sexuality in the relationship.
- Clarify roles within the relationship and delegate some of these to others.
- Establish healthy boundaries and roles in relationships.
- Think about what is important to deal with and ignore what is trivial.
- Talk about 'dreaded what ifs' as early as possible to help lessen fears and to clarify any wishes for later on in life.
- Avoid threats and ultimatums if things become intense and threatening; give yourselves the option of coming back to the issues later, or at least accepting that you do not agree over something.
- Avoid talking about sensitive issues at night and in bed, or in the bedroom!
- A couples or family therapist could be very helpful if you find that tensions frequently arise. Don't wait until the situation has deteriorated.

Most relationships undergo constant change in life, gradual or rapid. The advent of serious illness can lead to considerable changes in the beginning as the couple confront new challenges, but things may settle into a more stable and predictable pattern in time. Emotional, practical and even financial support from relatives, friends and employers can be of enormous help.

Not everyone who has cancer is in a couple relationship. Or, as is normal in everyone's life, some couple relationships will come to an end for a wide range of reasons. In some cases, this may be as a direct result of the illness. Some partners may feel overwhelmed by the situation and the unforeseen pressures. They may feel burdened by the different and/or extra demands placed on them. Some may become resentful of the intrusion of the illness into aspects of the relationship, including sexual intimacy, or find that the relationship has changed so much that it is completely different from where it was before the illness. John and his partner had to cope with complex and ongoing challenges to their relationship:

> My fiancée was treated for a brain tumour when she was 28. After extensive rehabilitation, she eventually managed to regain basic functions such as walking, talking and writing, things that most of us simply take for granted. It was not easy but we coped and our relationship survived. But she still bears the scars, both physically and emotionally.
>
> I don't care about her limp and I really don't care about the droop to the left side of her lips, but her temper tantrums and the bitterness have been difficult to handle. During these times, I have made persistent efforts to step into her shoes to gain an insight into the emotional pain she suffered; the loss of her old self, the fear of it happening again and the traumatic experience of waking up in the hospital with no feelings or movement in the left side of her body. It helped me to understand and it prevented me from personalizing her frustration. I have never doubted my love for her even when she doubted her love for me. I think that sometimes she was even testing me to see whether I truly loved her. There are times when she still struggles to accept the physical consequences of the tumour but the emotional scars are healing by the day.

Developing new relationships

How can one develop personal and intimate relationships while at the same time managing illness? How do we meet prospective partners and go on dates? How should we talk about our health condition, if at all? If we do so, how can the discussion develop in a way that builds hope for the future?

Dating or meeting a prospective life partner can be a challenge at the best of times. Here are some ideas, based on our clinical experience, for helping people develop new relationships:

- Be confident in yourself. Remind yourself that you are much more than your health problem or disability. Most people have something that they wish they could change, whether this is visible or hidden.

- Don't 'select yourself out' from finding the right person for you. This will become self-fulfilling and you will simply limit your options. Aim high.
- Switched-on people are attracted as much to a person's personality as to physical characteristics. Make both shine through. Emphasize your best features and characteristics. Focus on things that you can do and enjoy (not those that you can't).
- Convey confidence in living with and managing your condition. Show that you can cope and that others are not burdened by it. Speak confidently about your condition but don't let this part of the conversation dominate your time together. Be honest and realistic too. Talk about the impact it has on your life and how you manage it.
- Choose times carefully to introduce and talk about living with cancer. Sometimes this may not be possible when the effects are obvious or difficult to conceal. Avoid making it the first thing you talk about.
- Develop the conversation; there is no need to convey everything all at once in a first date. If there are sensitive areas that you feel you need to discuss, save these for later.
- Be patient and pace things appropriately. Accept that others may need some time to understand what you are experiencing and what it could mean for a relationship, and to gain the confidence that you have about living with the condition.
- Seek psychological counselling with an experienced practitioner to help you present a more confident side of yourself to others.
- Join a cancer support group. Others may have ideas for meeting a partner. Also, you never know who you may meet in such a group!

It is probably true for most people that a 'good' relationship takes time to develop, and may leave us feeling vulnerable and exhilarated at the same time. Having cancer adds a further dimension to the challenge of meeting someone and developing a new relationship.

If problems cannot be solved, it may be helpful to consult a therapist who specializes in working with couples coping with health difficulties. The effect can be to improve your understanding of what is happening in the relationship, open communication between partners and help resolve difficulties before they become entrenched problems.

9

Coping with advanced and terminal illness

From the start of a cancer diagnosis, almost everyone thinks of mortality and the possibility of dying. Even if treatment has been successful, many people with cancer live with the fear that it will come back. Receiving news that it has can be devastating and can have a far-reaching emotional impact on you and those around you. We often take our health for granted, so suddenly to be faced with our own mortality can completely alter how we see our future, our relationships and our finances.

Often, when cancer recurs, it is advanced – that is, it has spread from its primary site to other parts of the body. Advanced cancer is not uncommon, and sadly most people who die from cancer die because of the effects of advanced disease. While progressed disease is not usually curable, however, this does not mean it is always untreatable. People with advanced cancer may still have regular rounds of treatment, such as radiotherapy or chemotherapy, to keep their disease under control. Your doctors will continue to do what they can to ensure that your symptoms are managed appropriately so that your quality of life is affected as little as possible. The aspects of your care that focus specifically on treating pain, fatigue and other cancer- or treatment-related symptoms may become more important. With this type of holistic, palliative care, cancer can be treated for long periods of time.

Receiving bad news

It can be devastating to learn that your cancer has returned or progressed, or that it is so advanced that you will die from your disease. Such news will obviously affect different people in different ways, but for most people there will be a profound emotional impact.

You may feel shocked, stunned, tearful, angry or even confused. At the time, you may not be able to process the technical language about prognosis and survival that doctors are using, particularly if you are receiving bad news on your own. Many people have found it helpful to have a friend or family member with them at their appointments, to provide support and to ask questions or remember some of what has been said.

In their work, healthcare professionals sometimes have to deliver bad news to people. They have a responsibility to try and do this in a sensitive way that paints a realistic picture of the future, but the task is a difficult one and they may sometimes get it wrong. Surveys show that most patients want as much information as possible about their illness and the treatment options.[1] This is important, and the way news is given can have an effect on the way some people make an emotional adjustment to a diagnosis of cancer.[2] Most people want to be told the facts about their prognosis in a gentle, understanding way with a focus on what help is or will be available.

Karen's experience illustrates the immediate effects of hearing bad news. She was in her second year of remission when she discovered that her breast cancer had returned and spread.

Karen was stunned. She could feel the tears welling up but she found it difficult even to cry. Had she been naive, thinking her cancer had been cured? She thought back to her previous treatment and wondered whether there was anything else she could have done to prevent the recurrence. She tried to speak but her mouth felt dry and she could not think of anything to say. She sat in silence, waiting for her husband to pick her up from the clinic. How would she tell him? What would happen now? Could she possibly cope with the uncertainty of going through further treatment? Karen suddenly felt frightened: by the illness itself, the treatment and the effect it might have on her family. 'Why me? Sometimes it seems life is so unfair.'

A familiar face appeared around the corner – a warm hug and comforting words. Then the tears flowed and her emotions overwhelmed her.

Psychological reactions

Feelings of loss and grief are not reserved solely for the terminal stages of illness. They can be experienced in a wide range of situations following a diagnosis of cancer. We experience feelings of loss from the moment we contemplate the possibility or face the reality of serious illness. This may be in relation to loss of:

- predictable good health;
- bodily functions;
- status and role within a family;
- ability to relate freely to people;
- practical issues, such as one's ability to get in a car and visit relatives.

Given that loss can stem from so many different aspects of our life, it is sometimes an emotionally painful but helpful process to consider the ways in which loss affects us. It may then be easier to think of ways to compensate for certain losses and regain a level of functioning and some independence.

Experiences that are external to the cancer may accentuate the intensity of loss in your life. You may find it particularly difficult to cope with a child leaving home, for example, or a redundancy in the family, or divorce. These reminders of an uncertain future may feel just too much to bear when you are trying to accept the changes that lie ahead in your own life.

The topic of death and dying is, of course, a highly emotive one. Some people find it not only difficult to talk about, but also difficult to think about. There may be an underlying sense that doing so is tantamount to admitting that there is nothing that can be done to alter the course and outcome of illness, particularly when you have just heard that your cancer has advanced. The initial response is often a reluctance to accept the prognosis, though with time this may gradually become an awareness of what it means for you and your loved ones, and an acceptance of this future.

Your friends and relatives will be coping with the news in their own ways too. Some may show their reluctance to 'allow' their loved one to succumb to illness by encouraging you to fight on, to keep eating and by willing you to live. This can be stressful and upsetting for some people who, after extended periods of failing health, may 'welcome' the relief from pain and suffering. Even healthcare providers find it difficult to discuss end-of-life issues. It demands openness and a willingness to listen, and an ability to be receptive to other people's wishes, ideas, feelings and experiences. It also demands a great deal of empathy.

Some people who are terminally ill may be ambivalent about wanting to know what is happening to them and so may avoid direct conversation with their healthcare providers. A psychologist or counsellor who can facilitate such sensitive conversations can be especially helpful at such times, opening a discussion of matters such as how a person may wish to die, how he or she would most like to be remembered, and how beliefs and ideas about dying have evolved within the family, and undertaking a life review (see p. 78).

Impact on family and relationships

Death is part of the normal lifecycle: it is probably the most feared loss associated with a period of serious illness, although long-term disability and diminished health status, together with changed body image and a threat to one's predictable life, are also feared. The changes brought about by terminal illness can be made more complex and difficult if there are unresolved relationship problems within families. Besides this, terminal illness confronts family, friends and indeed healthcare professionals with thoughts and feelings about their own mortality.

Conversations about increasing dependency and about dying are very difficult for everyone. Yet at times they may be uppermost in the mind of a terminally ill person. Dependency issues may relate to activities such as going to the lavatory, bathing and brushing one's teeth. Some of these intimate tasks can be supported by nurses if the person is in hospital. However, if care takes place at home, it may fall to family, a community or district nurse or friends and relatives to help out. Open discussion about what is needed to facilitate these tasks may help to retain realistic hope and also a measure of dignity at a difficult time.

Pete, aged 62, was diagnosed with cancer of the colon. Following a number of tests, the medical team discovered that the cancer had spread to his liver. Did this mean that he was going to die? What was the prognosis? Pete felt that he needed to know as much as possible about his cancer, hoping that this would help both him and his family to prepare for the future. He made a list of questions to ask his doctor during his next visit to the clinic. Although the cancer was not curable, Pete was given information about various treatment options that might help to control the symptoms. The cancer growth was, unfortunately, rapid and Pete was told that he might experience some physical discomfort and fatigue within the next few months. Pete had been very worried that his cancer would leave him feeling weak and helpless, or even worse, that he would lose his independence and dignity. He found the idea of being physically dependent on his wife for basic functions such as feeding and going to the toilet deeply upsetting. He learned from the nurse specialist in the clinic that various cancer organizations offered professional care during the end stage of his illness. This was some relief to both Pete and his wife, who immediately contacted the Macmillan Cancer Support service to organize Pete's future care.

For Pete, it was important to learn that he did not have to depend wholly upon close family for intimate care. This helped to reduce his worry of losing his independence as he found the thought of accepting physical care from a professional easier to bear. This is not the case for everyone. Some people may find it difficult to rely on professional help and may prefer instead to be cared for by their family or friends.

Life review and spiritual dimension

In the search for certainty at a time when the future is so uncertain, many will seek solace in their religion. Others may for the first time in their lives ask questions about their spirituality. You may find yourself asking about the purpose of your life, about fate or about religion. Whether we do this consciously or not, a 'life review' is something that most of us undertake. These are some of the common questions that are asked:

• What sort of person was I?
• What did I achieve?

- How might I be remembered?
- How would I like to be remembered?
- What else or more might I have done?
- What if things had been different?
- What have I enjoyed?
- Whose lives have I touched the most?
- How have I lived?
- How have other people lived as a consequence of my life?
- What do I think happens to me in the next stage (perhaps invoking thoughts of an afterlife)?
- How might others cope and adjust without me? What do I wish for in their lives?

These are sensitive areas for reflection and are sometimes part of an internal conversation we have with ourselves. The process of a life review can also be an engaging and powerful way to communicate with loved ones around us.

Elizabeth had been living with terminal leukaemia for six months. At first she felt overwhelmed and depressed. She found it difficult to get dressed in the mornings and would often spend whole days in bed: 'What is the point if I am going to die?'

After she stopped attending clinic appointments, a clinic nurse helped Elizabeth recognize that she was not coping well with her illness and put her in touch with a counsellor. When the counsellor asked Elizabeth what she would most like to do in the remaining part of her life, her initial thought was that it seemed rather pointless as she most likely would die within the next year, but with the psychologist's help she came to understand that being diagnosed with terminal cancer had brought a sense of hopelessness that led her to abandon her dreams and wants. Although she would be unlikely to see her 17-year-old daughter get married one day, she would at least be able to take her family to the place in Paris where she first met her husband.

Planning

There are both practical and emotional challenges when we face life-threatening illness. One of these is to decide who is our next of kin and therefore has the right and privilege to help manage the terminal stage of illness and certain matters after death. The next of kin also have significant responsibilities, such as determining whether further medical support should be given.

Another consideration is the use of medication. Many of the symptoms associated with illness, such as pain, nausea and fatigue, can be uncomfortable. It is important to let your doctor and nurse know if you experience these as they can affect your mood, relationships and quality of life. Some people may decline the offer of drugs or other remedies, preferring instead to let the illness run its natural course. Careful consideration of what is most important for you may help you to prioritize how you would most like to cope.

Some people wish to prepare advance directives, legal documents that specify their wishes for medical care at the end of their life. 'Living wills', as they are sometimes called, provide an opportunity for people to decide in advance whether there are certain treatments they wish to refuse. Before drafting a directive, it is important to talk to those who love and care for you, and to a medical professional. A living will needs to be signed and witnessed, and copies should be left in your medical notes, with your doctor and with your next of kin.

Organizing and settling legal and financial matters can be necessary tasks in planning or preparing for the end of life. This is an area that should involve discussions with a lawyer, particularly if a will has not been drafted. While this is a practical issue, to leave such matters unsettled is an indirect message to others that we would prefer them to make decisions for us about our estate. However, this can ultimately give rise to conflict and further difficulties and is therefore best avoided.

There is also the challenge of considering your care during the closing stage of your illness. Although it may seem frightening having to think about where you would like to spend the final days of your life, choosing where to die is an important consideration that can help both you and your family and friends prepare for the end stage of your illness. Some people may choose to spend their last days at home surrounded by friends and family, while others may prefer to die in a hospital or hospice knowing that professional care is at hand. Whatever you decide is best for you, make sure to involve Macmillan nurses, the hospice or the hospital early on.

People will deal differently with the impending separation from those they love. Some may detach themselves in order to prepare for separation, while others may want to spend more time with friends and family. Ending relationships will take some sensitive consideration, and this can be particularly difficult when those relationships are with close family, including children.

A memory box, with childhood mementos, letters and personal reminders, is a popular way to leave tangible memories for those who love and support you, something they can read or touch or smell when they are thinking of you.

Massimo, diagnosed with pancreatic cancer six months ago, was feeling weaker and more exhausted by the day. He felt guilty that his wife, Elena, was left to care for their two young sons while he was lying in bed most of the day sleeping, and wished he could be more involved. It was difficult for Massimo to contemplate leaving his wife behind and to accept that he would never see his children grow up. He made Elena and each of the boys a 'memory box', containing pictures of their special moments together, birthday cards, drawings, personal letters for them and some of his own belongings, so that they would have tangible reminders of him throughout their lives. This, he felt, gave him a chance to share his memories with his family, and was something for the boys to take into the future that would remind them of the life they had with their father before he was ill.

Dying

One of the first questions that you may ask is about the circumstances that may surround your death. While your doctors may be able to give you some idea of your prognosis, improve your quality of life and treat symptoms and side-effects, they may never be completely certain when a person's life will end. Even if they are able to tell you how long you may live, you may feel too overwhelmed to apply what they are saying to your own life and circumstances. You will probably have many more questions than answers, and the uncertainty can be very difficult for you and your family, with many people feeling frightened and angry. Some books sensitively tackle these difficult issues; one example is *How to Approach Death* by Julia Tugendhat.[3]Always remember that there is no right or wrong way to face the situation.

Don't wait until the last moment to say goodbye. The people around you may be distressed or weary and may not have the capacity to engage. Saying goodbye can be done at any time and doesn't signal loss of hope or disrespect or tempting fate. Conversely, some who are suffering greatly with their illness may see death as a relief. They may be exhausted by the effect that cancer and the treatments have had on their bodies; for them, saying goodbye may be permission to stop fighting for life.

David Campbell, a well-known psychotherapist, has written a fascinating and illuminating piece about facing illness and the prospect of dying.

Dying

David Campbell

(Reprinted by kind permission of the author and first published as D. Campbell, 'Dying', *Context: The Magazine for Family Therapy and Systemic Practice in the UK* (2009) Issue 103, June.)

Following a major cancer operation, and chemotherapy that left the surgeons optimistic, my pancreatic cancer has metastasized and returned in the form of a tumour on my spine. This has been given palliative treatment with radiotherapy to 'stabilize' the tumour and reduce the constant back pain. But when the oncologists use terms like 'palliative' and 'stabilize' you learn pretty quickly that this is a cancer that will not now be cured ... at least by any known treatments. I have been referred to the Royal Marsden Hospital in Sutton to join a drug trial with some new drugs ... previously only tried on mice (which incidentally only gives me unexpected cross-species empathy for those little creatures ... 'Thanks, guys, for carrying the baton this far'). The consultant said there have been no advances in curing my type of cancer for the past 100 years ... and yet there must be some lingering hope somewhere, otherwise why would we all ... the drug companies, the mice, the medics and me ... be involved in this heroic exercise?

I am aware that I am writing this at a stage where I am still able to sit at the computer and still holding on to some hopes about treatments. One reason I am doing this is that it might help a reader or a therapist or a patient reconsider the taboos that we are so uncomfortable talking about. These are the territories where words prove their limitations and poets may be required, but I will try to put a few things down. At this time, much of my experience of dying is about keeping feelings manageable. There are times, like now, where I do want to try to make sense of what is happening to me, and there are times when I don't ... when I want distractions, such as the use of my omnibus collection of *New Yorker* cartoons, or a visit with a friend, or a film with my wife Jane. I can keep this compartmentalizing going reasonably well (is this a very male characteristic?) during the day, which is punctuated by patterns and routines, but life catches up with me at night, when I think about dying much more. There seem to be so many new feelings to process I hardly know where to begin. And, although I am sleeping less and much more lightly, it is rather comforting to have this time to myself. It is interesting that in my dreams, I am not represented as a patient dying of cancer, but as 'me', struggling with many other mundane obstacles. Then, when I wake, there are a few moments of stepping out of the dream before I fully wake up and say to myself, 'Oh yes, I forgot, I am actually in the real nightmare of dying of cancer.' So what do I think about it? It seems to be mainly about letting go. Letting go of everything that has made me what I am and everyone to whom I am connected. Closing the curtains to Jane, and the kids, and my friends and colleagues, every experience I have ever had, and every one of my responses to the world around me. Written like this, it seems impossible to contemplate, and I think it is, except brief glimmers during the day and night. I have been at the bedside when my mother and father and mother-in-law took their last breaths, and I imagine, like them, I will be drugged up, in and out of consciousness, and calm and quiet when the very end comes. And from a purely philosophical point of view, it's not possible to experience one's death if there is no 'experiencing being' switched on at the time. I can feel frightened, sad, hopeful, angry and resigned at different times ... it's confusing.

At the moment, I am keen to be in this world and to communicate, but I know that, as I get closer to death, I will lose interest in the world and begin to withdraw. I simply can't imagine what that will be like. I suppose it could be a comfort to relax and stop fighting against the inevitable, or it could be frightening to be aware of my family and the world drifting away. We'll have to wait and see.

I am afraid of too much sadness and of saying final goodbyes, of being conscious and having to look my family and friends in the eye knowing that I will never see them again. I have never had to face or even contemplate the idea of final, final goodbyes. Will I start crying and never stop, will I be crippled about the guilt of what I am leaving behind for my wife Jane and the kids? Will it be humiliating to lose too much control? Will I just drift away or will I be conscious of saying goodbyes? I think this may be the worst of all, having to look people in the eye and knowing I will be saying goodbye for the final time.

It is very hard to let go of the ultimate control of my life, when I have been proud of my ability to manage my life for so many years.

A large proportion of my time is spent not thinking about myself but about others and how they will manage. Things like: how will Jane cope with her grief, and will she be able to replace fuses and sort out pension payments, and will the kids manage good relationships and careers without me around to advise them? ... Not that my advice has made that much difference in the past few years. My struggle to leave things in good order is the counterbalance to the feeling that life, or death rather, is capricious and absurd.

I am not very good with pain but I can be very stoical about just enduring what life throws at me. I fear that I will cave in when the pain becomes too great and I will prove a fraud to myself and others for giving up and showing that I don't care as much about living, and all of you, as I make out to care. Up to a threshold, pain just has to be endured, but when it gets to the point where I cannot bear it any more it will be a sad day, because I know, while the pain can be dulled with drugs, it means that I have reached the end of a conscious, interactive life with others. It's like being at the top of a long slide I can remember from my childhood, and the pain eventually pushing me forward down the slide with the knowledge that that is my final experience ... So, fighting the physical sensation of pain is also a fight against the inevitable ending.

The answer to the rote question 'How are you?' becomes an exercise in mental gymnastics. Now, within a split second, I have to decide whether this person knows about my condition or not. If they don't, I have to decide whether to tell them, and in what level of detail, or whether to just give a perfunctory 'fine' and keep moving down the corridor. But if they do know what's happening, then I need to decide how current their news is, and again, I need to decide how much detail I want to discuss. In general, I am happy to describe my situation to anyone who is really interested ... it is morale-lifting. But, after discussing it with three or four people in a short space of time, that is usually enough. And I can see all this reflected on the faces of those I am speaking to. People aren't sure how much I want to say, and whether they are being intrusive or comforting, so they hold back a bit, perhaps waiting for me to take the lead. Possibilities for mis-connecting are myriad.

And what exactly can other people say? Some people present the positive hopeful view and may discuss diet and lifestyle changes; others will distract with talk about books or films, or exotic travels; 'Can I drive you to the hospital or make you a meal?' Others try to keep me connected to the outside world by giving me the juiciest gossip from work. And the point is that all of these conversations can be great or may just miss the point, depending on where I am at, and that can be difficult to judge, both for me and for others. I remember my dad, who ran the family funeral business for a period of time from age 19, saying, 'It doesn't really matter what you say as long as you are there.'

In the past, when I heard that someone of my generation had a life-threatening illness, I could hear myself saying. 'Whew, I'm glad it's him and not me' ... So I can only imagine that some people have a similar reaction to news of my cancer. And whether that encourages people to step away a bit, to avoid being contaminated by hopeless and helpless feelings, I'm not sure.

My hunch is that the reluctance that we all have to talk openly about dying is the fear of being overwhelmed by powerful feelings we have never before encountered: the rage at having everything taken away, and the awareness of ultimately being alone, and facing the lie that some things in life are permanent ... I do not want this piece to be about my speculations. I will leave that to others among you. I am well aware of the small guardians of taboo whispering to me not to go too far, but I wanted to contribute something to this topic by sharing some of my experiences so a reader will have a bit more understanding of what dying may mean.

Bereavement and adjustment

Some people never fully recover from the loss of someone they have loved dearly, and although they cope on a day-to-day basis they are forever affected by their bereavement. There is no expected or set pace at which life should return to 'normal' after someone close has died. It may be a very gradual process, and approaches from well-meaning friends who suggest that it is time 'to get on with life' may add to the distress.

For some bereaved people, one or more counselling sessions may help to clarify their thoughts and reassure them that their responses and feelings are normal. Support may be particularly welcome at certain times, particularly over special anniversaries such as birthdays, holidays and, of course, the anniversary of the death itself.

Bereavement and grief can have a profound impact on our psychological and physical wellbeing. It is important that people who have been bereaved give themselves time and don't deny the process they are going through. Emotions that have not been properly dealt with can return later, sometimes many years after the actual loss. Counselling can help to facilitate the expression of thoughts and fears that may otherwise not be spoken about. This is especially the case in families where death came suddenly or quickly, or where children are involved whose ways of coping with loss may be different from those of adults.

There are several good resources that some may find helpful in addressing the sensitive issues surround bereavement, including Geoff Billings' *Coping with Your Partner's Death: Your bereavement guide*.[4]

Some may experience a measure of relief when death finally occurs, ending both the person's suffering and the carer's distress associated with approaching loss. But death may also give rise to new and unanticipated problems for the bereaved, such as financial changes and unaccustomed self-dependency. Loss may also be complicated by the reality or fear of stigma when the cause of death is revealed. For example, cancer of the lung due to excessive smoking may carry with it an additional stigma not normally associated with loss.

Grief reactions may also be masked. If there is no open display of grief, it is difficult for others to know how a person is feeling and how to comfort or relate to them. Sometimes the bereaved continue to live as though the relative or friend has not died, or may find it too painful to think about, afraid of becoming overwhelmed by their feelings. If this is not addressed, it may be time to make an appointment to see a counsellor or psychologist.

Some people may never completely come to terms with the loss, particularly if it is the death of a partner or child. However, there is a clear difference between healthy mourning and that which comes to interfere with all aspects of functioning. As unpleasant as the feelings associated with loss are, they are normal. As one person whom we counselled once said, 'The price of love is grief.' This so aptly encapsulates everything we have tried to convey in this chapter. Emotional pain is something that we all experience when we lose a person we care for or about, and love.

The period of bereavement is a difficult and painful time for all concerned. Grief is a state and process that should never be rushed. The support of friends, family, loved ones, our religion or faith and, where required, a counsellor or psychologist, can help to make the feelings easier to bear.

10

Being 'a patient' and working *with* healthcare professionals

For most people, having cancer inevitably means developing a relationship with the healthcare system. For at least some of the time, you will be 'a patient'. What image comes to mind when you hear the term 'patient'? Do you have particular expectations associated with it? As patients, do we have different rights, different feelings towards or expectations of health providers and other people than when we are healthy? Does it change who we are or how we feel?

Being a patient in the twenty-first century is somewhat different from even a few decades ago. Health settings now try to be more patient-centred, and reflect the fact that treatment and care are more effective when patients are, and feel that they are, partners in their own care. Doctors strive to see the world through their patients' eyes, while patients are encouraged to be more involved in the way their illness is managed. We are given information about our condition, encouraged to join support groups, given a choice of places to receive our treatments, and may give feedback about our care. The internet also provides a way for patients to become 'experts' in their own condition. Treatment decisions should now be made in a transparent way. Nowadays, patients have access to their medical records and some doctors copy correspondence about patients to them as a matter of routine.

There are a number of important responsibilities that fall to us as patients. We are encouraged to be proactive and to understand our illness and the choices that are available to us. We need to navigate through the vast amount of health information that is available to everyone. We must also try and look after our health and wellbeing and manage some of the physical and emotional impact that cancer has, and know when to ask for help.

Finding and using information

Cancer treatments have advanced considerably in the last 50 years and new treatments are being developed all the time. We are also learning more about the causes of cancer and what we can do to prevent it in the first place. Hardly a day goes by without a news report of a ground-breaking discovery: a potential cure for some forms of cancer or a new treatment that will change your life. Those reading these reports may feel intense hope that a cure for their cancer is around the corner, but it is sometimes difficult to have a realistic sense of what this means for you.

When we are ill, information may take on additional importance. Our need to know what our symptoms mean and to find support can make us vulnerable. While there is some truth to the old adage that 'information is power', it has to be the *right* information and it has to be used *appropriately*. If you are looking for more information about cancer, here are good places to start:

1 *Your doctor:* consultations or appointments at the hospital or clinic provide an opportunity to ask questions and to clarify any issues about your condition.
2 *Cancer charities:* numerous cancer charities in the UK provide information and other support.
3 *Support groups:* these provide a place to share experiences and to learn new ways to cope with troubling feelings or symptoms. They also provide reassurance and enable us to improve our confidence in taking care of ourselves. Many cancer charities have local support groups across the country. Ask your doctor or nurse to recommend any relevant groups in your area, or call NHS Direct (0845 46 47).
4 *The internet:* an obvious source of information, this can also be a gateway to support groups or forums and other illness-specific resources that many people find helpful. You should, of course, be aware that the internet is a largely unregulated source of information.

Do see 'Useful addresses and finance' (p. 102) for further details.

Overall wellbeing

'Self-management' is a phrase often used by doctors and nurses to describe everyday approaches you can take to monitor and manage your symptoms, to deal with the emotional impact of illness, to adhere to your treatments and to look after your general health and wellbeing. The focus is on managing the condition and the effects it has on our lives. These effects are more than just physical or clinical. Some people talk about the need to consider the 'mind, body and spirit'. Several dimensions are important in this holistic approach to managing cancer, as depicted in Figure 10.1, and we discuss some of them in a little more detail in the sections that follow.

Diet

Diet is always an important part of health and wellbeing and remains so in cancer, which can affect your feelings towards food

Figure 10.1 Components of the holistic approach
Source: J. Cassidy *et al.*, *Oxford Handbook of Oncology.* Oxford University Press, Oxford, 2002.

in many different ways. Illness can suppress your appetite or may affect the way your body metabolizes food, so you may lose weight even if you are eating properly. Some cancers directly affect the digestive system, such as cancer of the oesophagus, stomach cancer, cancer of the colon or bowel cancer.

It is important to keep in mind general advice about a healthy, balanced diet. This includes:

- drinking sufficient water every day;
- eating the right balance of carbohydrates, fruit and vegetables, proteins and fats;
- avoiding excessive amounts of salt and sugar;
- avoiding too much alcohol.

Cancer Research UK provides a booklet of recipes and suggestions for appetizing meals for people with cancer (for contact details see p. 103).

Complementary and alternative therapies

Unlike some other cultures, Western culture is often described as regarding the body as being quite separate from thoughts and emotions. This is particularly evident in health care. Medical practice can reinforce this division by focusing on treating the physical aspects of illness in a way that often seems disconnected and isolated from other dimensions (thoughts, feelings, spiritual aspects). Some may feel that their deeper needs are neglected, particularly if they are facing serious or life-threatening illnesses. Many people with cancer seek out complementary therapies to supplement their traditional treatments, and these are increasingly offered alongside conventional support in cancer treatment centres across the UK.

The decision to use complementary therapies is an individual one. However, it is important that you involve your doctor in decisions about complementary treatments as some may be unsuited to particular cancers or certain treatments or drugs. Do bear the following in mind:

- Some people find relief from persistent symptoms through

complementary therapies. Good specialist cancer centres and charities can advise on suitable treatments.

- Complementary therapies are generally not as well regulated as traditional medical ones, so caution needs to be exercised about some claims made for such treatments. While regular medications must first be tested rigorously for efficacy and safety, this is not a requirement for most complementary treatments (including herbal medicines).
- On the whole, there is still limited scientific evidence for some complementary treatments. Better-conducted studies are needed before recommendations can be made on what is safe and effective, and to ensure that such treatments do not interfere with traditional treatments.

Exercise

Alongside a balanced diet, exercise helps keep weight down, keeps the heart healthy and can improve mood, confidence, sex life, sleep and quality of life as well as increasing levels of energy.

It should be safe for most people with cancer to exercise, although of course this will vary with the effects of treatment, your general fitness level, age and mobility. Whatever your cancer, take advice from your doctor as to whether you can exercise and what may be good for you in terms of levels of physical activity.

There are positive effects associated with regular exercise:

- Exercise can have a positive effect on your mood. Exercise encourages the brain to release certain chemicals, which can leave you feeling happier and more relaxed than you were before you worked out.
- Exercise delivers blood, oxygen and nutrients to your tissues and helps your entire cardiovascular system work more efficiently.
- Regular exercise can help you fall asleep faster and deepen your sleep.
- Exercise has a positive effect on your health, weight and overall vitality.

Expert patients

Clinical outcomes and quality of life may be improved by access to information and effective self management for a number of chronic conditions including cancer.[1] Expert patient programmes (EPPs) are courses designed for people who want to take a more active role in the management of their own condition. For more details, see <www.expertpatients.co.uk>.

Care in a hospice

Hospices provide treatment that focuses specifically on pain relief and other measures to improve quality of life (palliative care). Some people with cancer have medical and emotional needs that do not require the intensity and specialist care provided in a hospital. The treatments received in a hospice can complement medical care and can offer respite for carers. It is not true that hospices are just for the terminally ill, or are only places where people go to die. Some people attend day-care centres based in a hospice, returning home in the evening. Others may spend short periods of time there.

Some people nearing the end of their life may indeed wish to die in a hospice environment, and palliative care usually includes bereavement support for loved ones.

Your healthcare experience

There are a range of professionals involved in your care. You may find it frustrating having to tell your story over again to different people, and it may be upsetting to realize that you are just one among several patients your doctors are seeing. At times you may feel let down. It is easy to expect healthcare providers to be omnipotent and to treat and cure us, to communicate well and clearly, to give sound guidance, and to be empathic and understanding at all times, but doctors are only human and they can't be all these things all the time.

As you build up a relationship with your doctors, you will learn the best way to communicate. Communication is a two-way process. Your doctor will need to know what your symptoms are, how your medication is working and how you are coping. This information can only come from you. You, in turn, will rely on his or her expertise to allay your fears, to inform you of how cancer is affecting you and to keep you up to date with treatment options. You both have a responsibility to keep the communication channels open and the information flowing.

Any information we receive in a healthcare context can have an emotional effect. With cancer, we are often primed to expect bad news. This is certainly true when we are receiving a diagnosis, but can also be valid during treatment and follow-up. It is not easy to receive disappointing news about our health, but neither is it easy to give it, and some doctors do this better than others. In the context of being full participants in our healthcare decisions, we need to be informed about our treatment options, and this can only happen if we feel that information is given in a relevant and meaningful way. There are two sides to this: when we receive information we must be open to it, and the person providing the information must be knowledgeable and sensitive to how it will be received.

The following may be helpful ways to get the most out of your consultations with doctors and nurses:

- Write down questions in advance of appointments. When you see your doctor or nurse, having a list to hand can help jog your memory.
- Take in a notebook to write down answers to questions. Appointments can feel stressful and rushed and it may be difficult to remember what's been said. Ask your doctor or nurse to write some things down for you. Is there any printed information that you could take away with you?
- Consider taking a friend or family member with you for support and as an extra pair of ears.
- Importantly, don't feel disheartened if your doctor or nurse appears impatient. Doctors are busy and are under pressure to complete detailed forms and keep clinical records, and use of a computer often minimizes the amount of eye contact you have.
- If you feel unhappy with your care, try asking for more time

Box 2 Before you leave your appointment make sure you know the following

What might be wrong? You could ask the following questions:
- Can I check that I've understood what you said? What you're saying is …
- Can you explain it again? I still don't understand.
- Can I have a copy of any letters written about me?

What about any further tests, such as blood tests, scans and so on?
- What are the tests for?
- Who do I contact if I don't get the results?
- How and when will I get the results?

What treatment, if any, is best for you:
- Are there other ways to treat my condition?
- What do you recommend?
- Are there any side-effects or risks?
- How long will I need treatment for?
- How will I know if the treatment is working?
- How effective is this treatment?
- What will happen if I don't have any treatment?
- Is there anything I should stop or avoid doing?
- Is there anything else I can do to help myself?

What happens next and whom to contact:
- What happens next? Do I come back and see you?
- Who do I contact if things get worse? Do you have any written information?
- Where can I go for more information, a support group or more help?

or chatting with the person who referred you (your GP, for example). For more serious complaints, there is a formal system of recourse in the NHS and in private clinics. Most hospitals have a patient advice and liaison service (PALS).
- See 'Useful addresses and finance' for websites where you can find out more about your particular hospital and consultant.

The UK Department of Health has published a leaflet which aims to help people get the most out of their appointments.[2] Its suggestions are in Box 2.

Ask for help

We needn't always deal with challenges on our own. In fact, in many cases that won't be possible. It is important that we recognize when we need help and are able to ask for it.

There are several places to turn to for help. What suits you will depend on your personality and your particular challenges. Side-effects like nausea or hair loss are usually temporary but can be particularly distressing. There are treatments available for many such side-effects and you should talk to your doctor or nurse. With physical symptoms such as pain or fatigue, your coping thresholds may be more obvious to you, but with the other challenges, such as emotional ones, it is sometimes harder to recognize when help is needed. The majority of people manage well on their own and have no ongoing issues, but how do we know when we need help with our emotional problems? What might prompt the involvement of professionals?

The following might indicate that emotional support is needed:

- experiencing the same issues repeatedly;
- feeling that you need a fresh perspective;
- needing help for a specific challenge (e.g. coping with pain, sexual problems or relationship difficulties);
- experiencing persistent, very intense emotions (e.g. overwhelming feelings of depression, loss or fear);
- needing to pre-empt problems, especially those associated with difficult times;
- worrying about relationships, particularly if you feel you are to blame for relationship problems with loved ones or family members;
- promptings from other people: if people who care about you and who know you well suggest that you need help with some emotional difficulties, it may be time to consider their advice.

Receiving health care can be time-intensive. You may spend hours travelling to and from your doctor or hospital, waiting in queues,

Box 3 What is a clinical trial?

Before treatments (such as new drugs) are licensed to be given to patients, they must be tested thoroughly. This testing is done to prove that they are in reality effective (for example, that they do in fact slow the growth of cancer cells) and, importantly, to test whether there are any side-effects. The testing involves several different stages, usually starting with animal studies and then moving on to larger groups of human volunteers, before being tested in people with disease. New treatments are being tested all the time, particularly in fast-moving fields like cancer and HIV medicine. Patients being treated for cancer, for example, will often have the option of participating in a trial where they can be involved in the testing of an experimental treatment. If you are offered a place on a clinical trial, the drugs will have met a minimum threshold of safety and tolerability before they are tested on humans. It is important to remember, though, that because trials are comparing new treatments to old ones or to no treatment at all, not everyone in a study will get the new treatment.

Where to find out about trials

Your doctor will either have information about the ongoing trials that are relevant for you or should be able to tell you where to find it. Alternatively, there are resources available to patients on the internet: Cancerbackup (<www.cancerbackup.org.uk/Treatments/Trials/Understandingtrials>) not only provides an excellent and comprehensive explanation of what trials are, it also provides a database of current cancer trials that you can search according to the type of cancer you have.

waiting for referrals and test results and receiving chemotherapy. This inevitable waiting may lead to further distress. Friends or family who can accompany you to appointments can ease some of the burden and provide company on these occasions.

Be proactive

It is never easy to face up to and manage the realities of living with an illness, but people who are able to take a more active role in their self-management will have better outcomes in the long run. Being proactive in the context of illness is about acknowledging that you have a responsibility for aspects of your own health and wellbeing, and about making an effort to influence your experiences based on the choices that are available to you. One way to be proactive about your cancer is to keep up to date with medical developments and new treatments. Some medical trials may affect you. Clinical trials are medical studies of new treatments in patients. These are described in Box 3. Your doctor will almost certainly be aware of the trials that are most relevant to your type of cancer, so you can discuss these together.

What to expect from professional emotional support

Many cancer services integrate emotional support alongside medical treatments. While professional mental health support should be readily available, this doesn't mean that you automatically have serious mental health problems. Modern treatment centres recognize, however, that receiving a cancer diagnosis and coping with treatment can be stressful for you and your loved ones. The provision of mental health care is an option should you need it.

There are different groups of mental health professionals who approach treatment in different ways. Some explore experiences in your past and how these might impact on the way you're coping now. Other approaches are very client-centred, where providers are empathic listeners but offer little in the way of specific information or guidance. The aim is for you to feel listened to, in order for you to come up with your own solutions to your problems or issues. The approaches based on cognitive behavioural therapy (CBT) involve working towards a solution in partnership with your psychologist. This is a more scientific and rational approach to behaviour change, in line with the approach emphasized in this book. CBT may be short term or useful at different points or stages.

Other mental health professionals focus specifically on helping people with couple or family relationships. Family and couples therapists may or may not have specialist knowledge of cancer but will endeavour to focus on the impact of illness on close relationships.

Counselling can have different purposes and the approach should reflect your needs. Some counsellors provide information: facts about your illness, advice about test results, prevention strategies, information about treatment options and drug trials, etc. This is particularly relevant when the psychological supportive aspects of care are interwoven with the physical aspects of treatment, such as in oncology clinics. Other counsellors will discuss the implications of this information. They may discuss any lifestyle changes needed to accommodate your treatment regimens. In supportive counselling, the consequences – usually the emotional consequences – of the information are discussed. Psychotherapeutic counselling is more in-depth and focuses on healing, psychological adjustment, coping and problem resolution.

The authors of this book are experienced in all three approaches and use ideas and skills from all of them in their clinical work. We are often asked by people in cancer clinics: 'How will I know if my counsellor or psychologist or psychotherapist is helping me?' The simple answer is that if your specific problem or concern is being addressed and feels less of a challenge after sessions, then mental health care is probably working. If the focus of your sessions appears to have moved away from what is important to you, discuss your concern with your therapist. If you are not happy with how and where therapy is going, and you feel that your concerns are not being addressed, it is probably time to look for another therapist.

Some people may have the idea that counselling involves a long-term commitment with regular appointments. This needn't be the case. How often and for how long you see a psychologist or counsellor depends on what you want from the sessions and what your needs are. Sometimes a single session may be sufficient. Intermittent sessions with a therapist when the need arises may be the best model for most people. Other people may prefer regular sessions so they are assured of a more constant external emotional support system.

A good therapist will work hard to understand what you do well. He or she will build on your strengths and will work with you in your context to help find a way to minimize the negative impact of your illness on your life. See 'Useful addreses and finance' for more information on getting emotional support.

Further reading

Coping Successfully with Pain, Neville Shone (Sheldon Press, 2002)
Coping with Bowel Cancer, Dr Tom Smith (Sheldon Press, 2005)
Coping with Breast Cancer, Dr Terry Priestman (Sheldon Press, 2006)
Coping with Chemotherapy, Dr Terry Priestman (Sheldon Press, 2009)
Coping with Radiotherapy, Dr Terry Priestman (Sheldon Press, 2007)
Reducing Your Risk of Cancer, Dr Terry Priestman (Sheldon Press, 2008)

Useful addresses and finance

A word about information

It is important that we don't take everything we read at face value. A little scepticism will help us to navigate information with greater confidence and authority. Ask yourself:

- Who wrote this?
- Are they an expert?
- Have they any unstated or vested interests?
- What is underpinning this piece? (Evidence, opinion, a random word generator?)
- What do other people think about this source?
- What is my response to what I am reading?
- Do other sources say the same thing?
- Am I being asked to part with any money?

General health information and support

BBC Health
Website: www.bbc.co.uk/health
Provides information on a range of conditions.

Dipex
A registered charity that runs the website <www.healthtalkonline.org>. This is an excellent information site. You can watch and listen to people talking about a variety of illnesses and share your own experiences.

'Dr Foster' (www.drfosterintelligence.co.uk)
This site provides a hospital guide and a guide to consultants.

Healthcare Commission (www.healthcarecommission.org.uk)
This organization publishes information about different hospitals, NHS and private.

The National Health Service (www.nhs.uk)
This is a comprehensive health website. You can also search for services (carers, support for independent living, GPs, walk-in centres, screening), information and support groups. The website also contains a searchable hospital database with information about your local hospital, such as the quality of care, and other important considerations such as how clean it is.

NHS Direct
Tel.: 0845 46 47 (24-hour helpline)
Website: www.nhsdirect.nhs.uk

Patient UK (www.patient.co.uk)
This site is largely written and edited by GPs.

Specialist information and support

Cancer Research UK (CRUK)
61 Lincoln's Inn Fields
London WC2A 3PX
Tel.: 020 7121 6699 (supporter services)
Website: www.cancerresearchuk.org

CRUK also runs the patient-information website <www.cancerhelp.org.uk>. Contact CancerHelp's team of cancer specialist nurses between 9 a.m. and 5 p.m., Monday to Friday, on 020 7061 8355; freephone 0808 800 4040.

Macmillan Cancer Support
89 Albert Embankment
London SE1 7UZ
Tel.: 020 7840 7840; helpline: 0808 800 4040 (for information, questions and support)
Website: www.macmillan.org.uk/Home.aspx

Maggie's Centres
The Stables, Western General Hospital
Crewe Road
Edinburgh EH4 2XU
Tel.: 0131 537 2456
Website: www.maggiescentres.org

A Maggie's Centre is intended to be a kind of one-stop-shop for any problem, large or small, associated with cancer: help with benefits, psychological support (one-to-one or in groups), stress-reducing strategies, and support and help for those involved in caring as well as those with cancer. Appointments don't have to be made, nor is referral necessary, and it is all free. The Edinburgh one was the first, but there are now several others in England and Scotland (the website provides further details), and more are planned, including one in Barcelona and another in Hong Kong. Even the buildings are specially designed to induce a sense of calm and welcome.

Hospice care

Help the Hospices
34–44 Britannia Street
London WC1X 9JG
Tel.: 020 7520 8200
Website: www.helpthehospices.org.uk

The leading charity supporting general hospice care throughout the UK, Help the Hospices can provide information on individual hospices. Some hospices are run by charities, including Marie Curie Cancer Care and Sue Ryder Care. There are NHS-run hospices and palliative care teams in NHS hospitals.

Counselling and support

Association for Family Therapy (AFT)
Tel.: 01925 444414
Website: www.aft.org.uk
Based in Warrington, AFT is the leading body representing those working with families in the public and independent sector in the UK. The broad group of therapies under the banner of 'systemic family therapy' work not only with families but with individuals and couples.

British Association for Counselling and Psychotherapy (BACP)
15 St John's Business Park
Lutterworth
Leics LE17 4HB
Tel.: 01455 883300 (general enquiries); 01455 883316 (Client Information Helpdesk)
Website: www.bacp.co.uk
The membership organization of registered counsellors and psychotherapists in the UK. There is a searchable database, or the Client Information Helpdesk seeks to help with what might appear to be the daunting prospect of choosing a counsellor or psychotherapist matching the needs of the individual.

British Psychological Society (BPS)
St Andrew's House
48 Princess Road East
Leicester LE1 7DR
Tel.: 0116 254 9568
Website: www.bps.org.uk
BPS is the professional association for academic, clinical and other chartered psychologists, as well as being the representative body for psychology and psychologists in the UK. Lists of psychologists and free advice and information leaflets may be downloaded from the website.

Institute of Family Therapy (IFT)
Tel.: 020 7391 9150
Website: www.instituteoffamilytherapy.org.uk
Situated in London, IFT is the largest family-therapy organization in the UK, providing clinical services for families and couples.

UK Council for Psychotherapy
Second Floor, Edward House
2 Wakley Street
London EC1V 7LT
Tel.: 020 7014 9955
Website: www.psychotherapy.org.uk
This Council is the umbrella body for all psychotherapy practised in the UK, with more than 70 training and listing organizations in its membership. It provides directories of psychotherapists, information on different types of talking therapies and guidance on how to choose a therapist.

Finances
Finances will be a worry for many people living with cancer. Until April 2009, people had to pay towards the cost of their medications, and there are other costs, such as travel to and from appointments, parking at most hospitals and clinics, and childcare. Some people may need to reduce their working hours, at least during treatments, or stop work altogether.

Prescription charges
From April 2009, people taking cancer drugs can apply for a five-year exemption from prescription charges. Application forms are available through GPs and oncology clinics. For those who have already bought a prescription payment certificate (a more cost-effective way of buying prescriptions if you need more than three of them in three months or more than 14 over 12 months), you can apply for a refund when you get your new exemption certificate.

Housing costs
If you can't work, the costs associated with staying in your home – be that a mortgage, rent or bills – may be one of your biggest worries. There are benefits available to help and you may be eligible. Housing benefit, which includes a local housing allowance, extends to private tenants on low incomes whose savings fall below a certain threshold. Check with your local authority for details.

Council tax benefit help people on a low income to pay their council tax. This is an income-related benefit and your hospital, cancer charities or your local authority will have more information.

Travel
If you (or your partner) are on a low income or are receiving income

support, Jobseeker's Allowance, a guarantee credit of pension scheme, working tax credit or, sometimes, child tax credit, you may be eligible for help with train or bus fares, or with petrol costs associated with travel to hospital. This may also extend to people who travel with you. The system can be quite complicated, but your hospital or clinic should have information about whether you are eligible and how to make a claim. Always keep copies of your travel receipts as you'll need these to claim the costs back.

Community transport schemes, such as Dial-a-Ride, may be available in your area. They run a car service during working-week hours which can take you door to door if you have difficulty using public transport. If you receive incapacity benefit or severe disability allowance, then you may be eligible for this scheme. However, different geographical areas have different eligibility criteria, and it may be best to telephone a cancer charity (see earlier in Useful addresses and finance) for more information. In London, Dial-a-Ride is provided by Transport for London (020 7222 5600; www.tfl.gov.uk).

Taxicard is a scheme run by boroughs in London which allows you to take subsidized taxi journeys. People with a long-term impairment in mobility who live or work in London are eligible for this service (020 7934 9791; www.taxicard.org.uk).

Help with your children
Child tax credits are for people aged at least 16 who are responsible for at least one child who is in full-time education. You may also qualify for help towards childcare. If you are on a low income, you may be entitled to help with clothing and school meals. Your children are entitled to free school meals if you receive income support, income-based Jobseeker's Allowance or in some cases child tax credit. You can check your eligibility and apply for this through your local authority.

Support for carers
Carers can sometimes be the 'unsung heroes' in the face of cancer. If you have someone caring for you while you are ill, ask your local social services departments what help they provide. They should be able to arrange an assessment.

Carers over 16 who do more than 35 hours' caring a week may be eligible for a carer's allowance. Speak to a benefits adviser at a cancer charity or have a look at the benefits information on the official government website (www.direct.gov.uk).

Macmillan, who has now joined forces with Cancerbackup, provides a booklet for carers called 'Hello, and How Are You?' See more about it on their website <www.macmillan.org.uk/HowWeCanHelp/Publications/MacmillanPublications.aspx>.

Wigs and fabric supports
For people with hair loss, the cost of wigs can be prohibitive. Free acrylic wigs or fabric supports are available for certain people through the NHS.

Statutory Sick Pay (SSP)
SSP should be available to anyone under a contract of service, who is sick for four or more days in a row and who is also earning at least £90 per week. The current rate (April 2009) of SSP is £79.15 per week; it starts from your fourth day of sickness and is paid for a maximum of 28 weeks.

Grants from charities
Macmillan and some other charities offer one-off grants to some people affected by cancer. Eligibility depends on weekly household income and individual savings, and you need to apply through a health or social work professional (district nurse, Macmillan nurse, social worker).

Further financial information
In general, if you are under 60 years old, your eligibility for cost exemptions and help with additional costs, such as travel, depends primarily on your level of income and the other benefits you might be receiving. You can find more comprehensive information through the following:

Macmillan Cancer Support has a financial support section (www. macmillan.org.uk/HowWeCanHelp/FinancialSupport/FinancialSupport. aspx). There is also a publications section (http://be.macmillan.org. uk), which provides an excellent booklet, 'Help with the cost of cancer'. The Macmillan Benefits Helpline (0808 808 2020) enables you to speak directly to a benefits adviser.

Call the Benefits Enquiry Line (a non-governmental organization) on 0800 882 200 for advice on benefits for patients, disabled people and carers.

The booklet HC11 ('Help with health costs') is available from your hospital, GP or clinic. Search the government website <www.dh.gov.uk> for 'HC11'.

Postscript

We set out to share our experiences of working with people affected by cancer. Since no two people and situations are the same, only some of the ideas that we discuss may be relevant to you and to your circumstances. We have tried to avoid being prescriptive about how to best cope with cancer but instead have highlighted the main emotional effects of illness and treatment on the individual, couple relationships and the family. We have also addressed the relationship between you and your professional carers.

We have taken a practical approach, emphasizing what you can do to cope better, but this should not be construed as over-simplifying illness. In the face of significant challenges brought about by chronic or acute conditions, it is important to gain some clarity about what you are confronting and how you feel, how this impacts upon you and your relationships, and how best to marshal your resources to cope. We hope that this book goes some way to helping you to achieve this and that it provides a resource to accompany you in difficult times.

Notes

2 The emotional impact of cancer

1 Adapted from A. Faulkner and P. Maguire, *Talking to Cancer Patients and Their Relatives*. Oxford University Press, Oxford, 1994, cited in C. A. White, *Cognitive Behavioural Therapy for Chronic Medical Problems: A guide to assessment and treatment in practice*. John Wiley and Sons, Chichester, 2001.

3 Regaining control

1 D. Burns, *The Feeling Good Handbook*, second edition. Plume, USA, 2000.
2 Deborah Hutton, *What Can I Do to Help?* Short Books, London, 2005.

9 Coping with advanced and terminal illness

1 P. Schofield *et al.*, 'Hearing the bad news of a cancer diagnosis: the Australian melanoma patient's perspective', *Annals of Oncology* (2001) 12: 365–71; V. Jenkins *et al.*, 'Information needs of patients with cancer: results from a large study in UK cancer centres', *British Journal of Cancer* (2001) 84(1): 48–51.
2 C. Roberts *et al.*, 'Influence of physician communication on newly diagnosed breast patients' psychological adjustment and decision making', *Cancer* (1 July 1994) 74 (1 Suppl.): 336–41.
3 Julia Tugendhat, *How to Approach Death*. London, Sheldon Press, 2007.
4 Geoff Billings, *Coping with Your Partner's Death: Your bereavement guide*, Sheldon Press, London, 2008.

10 Being 'a patient' and working with healthcare professionals

1 A. Coulter and J. Ellins, *Patient-focused Interventions: A review of the evidence*, Picker Institute Europe, 2006, available from <http://www.health.org.uk/publications/research_reports/patient focused.html>.

2 Department of Health, *Questions to Ask: Getting the most out of your appointment*, available from <www.dh.gov.uk>.

Index